CRITICAL ACCLAIM FOR *AS THE CROW FLIES*

Ed Hudson does a superb job of relating Freddie Crow's intriguing life from both a law enforcement and personal perspective. Although not necessarily a faith-based story, it is a story of redemption nonetheless. *As the Crow Flies* promises to be a satisfying *page turner* and one that leaves the reader, and pilots in particular, a desire to learn more about these risky vignettes.

PAUL ENTREKIN, Author of *Mighty Hands:
Victory over Adversity Through the Grace of God*, and
Mr. MiG: And the Real Story of the First MiGs in America

As the Crow Flies is a gripping read about a likable hard-charging drug smuggling pilot. Ed Hudson's book details true circumstances involving a complex action-packed drug smuggling investigation in a compelling manner. As the story develops, the reader is drawn to understand ramifications between family members and loved ones of the criminal offender. Interactions between the lawman and former drug smuggler lead to a faithful and uplifting end.

FLOY TURNER, Best-Selling Author and Special Agent,
Retired, Florida Department of Law Enforcement

Ed Hudson does a great job sifting through the job of a law enforcement officer and the human lives of the people he pursues in his profession. Being a cop in a small town is not easy. The people you deal with are sometimes your friends. Everybody has a job to do. The book shows the compassion and forgiveness between the hunter and the hunted. *As the Crow Flies* brings it full circle showing how friendships develop in the most unsuspecting ways. Great read.

JOE THOMAS
Publisher, *Tri-City Ledger*
Flomaton, Alabama

As the Crow Flies

The Redemption of an International Drug Smuggler

Ed Hudson

STOREHOUSE
MEDIA GROUP
Your Book...Your Voice...the World!

DISCLAIMER FROM THE AUTHOR

I have tried to recreate events, locations, and conversations from my
memories of them, as well as from police reports, court transcripts,
and newspaper articles. While all of the events did occur in
Northwest Florida, some locations, as well as the names and
identifiers of some individuals in the book, may have been changed
to maintain their anonymity and protect their privacy.

Paperback ISBN: 978-1-943106-55-4
E-book ISBN: 978-1-943106-56-1
LCCN: 2020915497

Photo of the author by Kirsten McCall Photography.

Printed in the United States of America

1 3 5 7 9 10 8 6 4 2

As it is written, There is none righteous, no, not one:

ROMANS 3:10

Contents

Foreword

Popular culture tends to classify everyone into neat categories, ascribing the same characteristics to everyone in each category. The category of criminal conjures up the picture of an unrepentant villain who is evil to the core. A certain percentage of criminals are psychopaths, but my career as a criminal trial lawyer taught me that most criminals aren't much different from anyone else except that they tend to choose socially unacceptable solutions to difficult problems.

We all contend daily with a force inside us that Sigmund Freud labeled the id, but that St. Augustine centuries before called Original Sin. The Apostle Paul summed up that inner contest with the words "The good that I would I do not, but the evil which I would not, that I do." Criminals tend to lose this inner battle more often and more spectacularly than average people. This battle between the good that we would and the evil we would not is often compromised when we convince ourselves that the minor evil we contemplate will serve a greater good.

This book tells the story of one man's struggle to achieve what he thought to be the greater good of prosperity for himself and his family by committing the lesser evil of drug smuggling. It is a story which resonates with me on at least three levels—on one level because during my years of service as a drug prosecutor I came to know many drug smugglers on a professional basis; on another level because during most of the time that I prosecuted drug smugglers my brother smuggled drugs; and on a third level because it is the universal story of sin, loss, repentance, and redemption.

Some look at the typical drug smuggler as irredeemably evil, like Al Pacino in *Scarface*. Others might think the smuggler a sort of modern-day Robin Hood, like Robert Mitchum in *Thunder Road*. My thirty years of experience as a prosecutor leads me to believe that the average drug smuggler is more like Jerry Orbach in *The Gang that Couldn't Shoot Straight*. One of my first drug smuggling cases involved a young kid who was working his way through college hauling loads of marijuana along Florida's Interstate Highway system. He chose to pursue the greater good of a college degree by the route of what he believed to be the "lesser evil" of drug smuggling.

I first became aware of Freddie Crow when Freddie and my brother both got arrested for conspiracy to smuggle drugs. This arrest represented the nadir of their years-long careers as drug smugglers— careers in which they had reaped fabulous wealth, increasingly long prison sentences, and anguish for those who loved them. Both Freddie and my brother came from similar backgrounds, and both faced similar choices at the beginning of their smuggling careers. Both took the path of lawlessness for much the same reasons, and the paths they chose eventually came to another milestone where they were presented with another choice.

Freddie and my brother made different choices at this second milestone, and their lives took different paths afterward. They were confronted with the question, "Should I cooperate with law enforcement and testify against my accomplices?" I used to tell defendants who were contemplating such a decision that they had an opportunity to dissociate themselves from the life of crime that they had been leading and set themselves on the road to rehabilitation. Many defendants agreed to testify; most of them later returned to a life of crime. Freddie chose to testify; my brother refused. Freddie received ten years; my brother got life without parole.

In an effort to win that inner contest between good and evil, Freddie chose what he considered the lesser evil of betraying his friends in order to pursue the greater good of putting his life back together and atoning for the pain he had caused his loved ones. My brother preferred the greater evil of a Draconian sentence to the lesser evil of betraying his friends. Although Freddie Crow is the focus of this book, we learn the eventual consequences of both choices.

George R. Dekle Sr.
Final Prosecutor of Ted Bundy, and author of
Prairie Defender: The Murder Trials of Abraham Lincoln;
The Lindbergh Kidnapping Case: A Critical Analysis of the Trial
of Bruno Richard Hauptmann; Cross-Examination Handbook:
Persuasion, Strategies, and Techniques; The Last Murder:
The Investigation, Prosecution, and Execution of Ted Bundy

Acknowledgements

I would like thank Freddie's family—his wife Sandra and sisters Bobbie and Tricia—for all of the support they have given me in this endeavor. Each one has been more than open about the events that have occurred and the way they have affected their lives. I know the questions I asked them were sometimes difficult to answer simply because of the memories they invoked.

I also must thank Christina Camac for all of her proofing and encouragement over the months of writing. Her assistance helped me to provide the best product I could to present to the wonderful people of Storehouse Media Group where Sherrie Clark developed it into the book you see.

Lastly, I would like to thank my wife Sharon. She opened her home to a former international drug smuggler. Sharon chose to get to know him rather than judge him. She understood my need to help him, and when it came time to write the book, she offered so much encouragement.

Introduction

I have long felt that we all have at least one book inside of us. A compilation of events, places traveled, people met, and circumstances unique to every individual from whom we could all learn.

During my thirty-four years of service in law enforcement, I have come across just those types of circumstances I thought would result in a book worth reading, and I had considered writing a book, just not this book. If someone had told me ten years earlier that I would be writing this book, I would have thought they had lost their mind.

Getting to know Freddie Crow and his family and seeing the impact he left in people's lives changed my mind. This is a story of the redemption of a man who lived life in the fast lane and sought thrills that could only be obtained in the sky on an airplane with 800 pounds of marijuana all around him. It's the once-conflicting story of a man who was simultaneously generous to others but oftentimes put himself first.

All of this would change when everything was at risk. Freddie's eyes would open to the consequences of his actions and what they had done to his family and to himself. The true Freddie Crow would learn to put others first and to beg God and his family for forgiveness. Only then was he ready for the one true love of his life—Sandra.

This book is also the story of opposing sides coming together as if directed by God. It is the story of a friendship where one friend walked the other through death's door, helping him to prepare along the way. It is a story, I became convinced, that was worth telling.

I attempted to maintain a factual basis by using court transcripts, police reports, newspaper articles, and personal recollection. Still, so many others have stories concerning Freddie and their relationships with him that have not been included in this book. I did not intend to slight anyone because I know their stories and relationships are just as important. His life was full of stories. Some of them I know, and many of them I don't. I can only hope I have done his life justice.

It is my desire that everyone get something out of this book. For those who knew Freddie, I hope it brings back fond memories. For those who didn't know Freddie, you will by the time you finish reading this book.

Chapter 1

As the Crow Flies

It would have been a perfect day for the beach, the kind of day where the warmth of the sun came flowing through the cockpit, and the reflection bounced off the water like a bright light shining through broken glass. When flying over the beaches of Mexico, it was entirely too easy to lose one's self; however, becoming distracted was not something a pilot could afford to do. After all, no one knew better than Freddie Crow just how important staying alert was. Eight hundred pounds of marijuana called for undivided attention, even before taking possession of it. Then once the plane landed in Belize, Central America and contact was made on the ground, the tension would begin to mount.

This day started fifteen hours earlier. The plane had been fueled, and all of the preflight checks were made before leaving the Florida Panhandle. This particular plane had never been used. It was kind of "on loan," so to speak, which was another way to say it had been stolen. Several days in advance, the plane had been taken from a small airstrip late at night when no one was around.

Since these small airplanes were easily started with a common key, all that was required was choosing the proper time, usually at night, and then the right amount of courage. Once the plane was obtained, whether stolen or legitimately borrowed or purchased, it would be taken to a secure location where all of the seats except the pilot's would be removed. The bladder tanks would be installed for the long trip. Freddie was fortunate to be in an organization that took care of all this. His job was to fly and make the deals, and those were tasks he did very well.

Flying out of the country was a rather simple process since no one seemed to care when it came to the small planes. Detailed plans had to be made, from preparing the plane all the way to offloading it. The entire process took coordination with the supply source, readying the plane for the trip, lining up distributors, and hopefully picking a day with the right weather—an overcast day with no moon at night.

Everything must be considered to avoid detection, which meant reducing the chances of light reflecting off your plane. Today was supposed to be a day like that, but a dependable weather day for flying was much like depending on the weather for anything else.

As Freddie looked through the cockpit window, he noted how the sky just happened to clear out. While this would have made for a rather enjoyable trip to Belize, it wasn't the type of day he was looking for. However, according to Freddie, any day in a plane was better than a day in the office, even if he didn't actually know what a day in the office was like.

The flight to Belize could be very relaxing, but there was a quickening of the pulse upon approach. The landing at a remote strip in a foreign country to conduct illegal activity had a way of getting the adrenalin flowing.

Freddie always tried to choose trustworthy people to deal with, but when you're involved in an illicit business, one can never be too careful. He was always happy to get the plane fueled and loaded and then get right back into the air; however, that didn't always happen so easily.

The desire to pack the plane sometimes came into conflict with the laws of physics. Too much marijuana made for a precarious or impossible takeoff on short runways. Sometimes the weight of the load would cause the doors on the plane to fly open, and it didn't take an expert to know the doors didn't need to be open in the air. For this reason, the pilot had to resist the lure of increased profits and refrain from overloading the plane.

So far, this had been a good trip. The plane was loaded with marijuana stacked behind him, beside him, and even up on the dash, and Freddie was on his way home. A small opening right in front of him allowed him to see everything he needed to see. The smell? Well, that was something one just had to get used to.

In addition to these conditions, the length of the day made it hard to stay focused as it wore on. The adrenaline rush was no longer necessary because this part of the trip came with less worry; he could allow his mind to drift off. At times like this, he began to think about how a boy from Century, Florida, could wind up in this kind of a situation.

He had loved to fly since his teenage years, partially from the freedom he felt in the air, but mostly from the excitement he could obtain from controlling an airplane as well. Undoubtedly, that same excitement was what brought him to smuggling marijuana. The money was good, but it had never been about the money. His father could have kept him in enough money to do what he wanted, but where was the excitement in having money given to you?

The idea of pushing the envelope, of getting away with something that others would like to prevent you from doing had always appealed to him. There was just something about living on the edge that really gave meaning to his life.

Unfortunately, this type of lifestyle did not come without cost—first and foremost, being captured by law enforcement. Freddie had already experienced state and federal prisons for past drug-related misdeeds. Although not fun, somehow his time in captivity seemed to make him long for excitement even more. To get out a free man and have the opportunity to once again pursue those adrenalin surges seemed to be more than he could control.

If the fear of incarceration was the only drawback, then he wouldn't have a cause for concern. It was the other costs that gave him trepidation and those "what if's" that nagged him from time to time.

Freddie loved airplanes, but he didn't have to end up here, smuggling marijuana. He had heard about bush pilots in Alaska, who flew over rough topography without any man-made runways to land the plane. The thought of being surrounded by beautiful country, combined with his natural love for hunting and fishing, should have made Alaska the goal of his life. Alaska had so many locations where the airplane was the exclusive means of travel, so becoming a bush pilot would have locked him in for a perfect fit. But Alaska was far, far away, and he just hadn't made it there yet. Maybe one day he could go there and start all over again. For now, it could remain a dream.

No, it was not even Alaska that made him question his place in life so much; it was family. Freddie was not lost on what his actions had done to them. His oldest sister Bobbie had tried so hard to make him turn his life around. She was almost twelve years older than Freddie and remained the one person who looked after him for his entire life.

For the last forty years, from his birth until now, she had always been there to help him. She, more than anyone, wanted the best for him.

If these second thoughts and troubling considerations weren't enough, his younger sister Tricia was married to the Alabama State Trooper Harry, who didn't even like to think about what Freddie did for a living. Freddie's older brother Hurston had worked his way up in the United States Forest Service, so he also couldn't afford to be linked to an international smuggling ring.

Then he had nieces, whom he dearly loved and who loved him unconditionally, although at times their disappointment in his actions showed through. However, Bobbie was still the one he most hated to disappoint. Her tears would soak through to his soul and leave him at odds with himself.

Realizing his mind had drifted to a place he didn't need to be, Freddie began to refocus on the task at hand. He would often rationalize whether his actions were really that wrong. It was only marijuana.

Without a doubt, he would see this natural weed become legal one day soon, so all he was really doing was getting ahead of the curve. Other countries had legalized marijuana, and hell had not broken loose yet. Marijuana had even proven to be of some value as medicine. Some of the medications doctors prescribed now certainly resulted in bigger problems than marijuana could ever cause.

The continued prohibition of marijuana just didn't make sense to him, but that's just the way it was. After all, if marijuana was legalized, then the thrill of smuggling would be gone, and right now, that was his driving force.

At the moment, what *was* important was hitting the proper longitudinal line from the Yucatan Peninsula and flying over to the latitudinal line leading up to the Big Bend area of Florida. His plane had radars to avoid, and Freddie had mastered this technique.

He used to worry about the ground crew being on time at the right place. Nothing could ruin a good trip more than making it all the way back to the strip and having no one there to unload. For that reason, he had elected to pay the offload crew very well for their participation. Fifteen thousand dollars a load was a lot of money to pay each crewman, but it ensured dependability and took the worry out of this part of the operation.

Also, he was fortunate enough to have a partner who flew in loads, which assured the organization of an income so that money was never an issue. However, in some ways, money had become a problem. Without a good way to launder it through a business, Freddie was unable to deposit the proceeds into a bank account. For this reason, he chose to bury money in PVC pipes in various undetectable locations. Now all that was left was remembering the locations, and that, he feared, was already a problem.

Once the money was buried, he tried not to go back to its location. He didn't necessarily need the money because it continued to flow in, but still, he had to fight the urge not to go back to just check on it. Someone might see him. Nevertheless, wooded locations had a way of constantly fluctuating. Trees fell, limbs blew down, and the whole terrain could be altered. If these changes weren't kept up with through constant visitations, then the area could become unfamiliar.

In the meantime, Freddie continued to fly across the Gulf of Mexico to the point where he needed to turn north toward the Big Bend. This route would help him avoid the radar of Eglin Air Force Base in Okaloosa County, Tindall Air Force Base in Bay County, and MacDill Air Force Base in Tampa.

Work still needed to be done. Coming in at the right location was only half of it. The rest was the tricky part, which required a pilot skill not many could match, and those who could do it probably wouldn't want to. But this was the part that motivated Freddie Crow and separated him from most. Soon, he would begin flying so low to the surface that salt from the sea spray would collect on the windshield, decreasing his already-limited view.

The early days of flying as a crop-duster fresh out of high school helped prepare Freddie for this endeavor. Crop-dusting is a method of spraying chemicals onto agricultural products, such as corn, soybeans, and cotton, by flying sometimes a quarter of a mile or longer over the planted field. As the plane approaches the field to be sprayed, it takes an acrobatic dive until skimming mere feet over the crop. Right at the end of the field, the plane takes a sweeping climb upwards, narrowly avoiding trees or power lines while simultaneously cutting the spray on and off at just the right time.

Many accidents have happened in this profession. Flying so low to the ground has made for some very bad crashes, with some folks being lucky enough to walk away. It takes a very good pilot to crop-dust, but Freddie wasn't crop-dusting now. He was drug smuggling over the ocean, and its waves didn't stay motionless like agricultural products in a field. Its wind could be extremely challenging to maneuver in at times, especially when flying so low over the waves in 200-mile stretches. If you crash while flying here, there's not much left to do but drown, ending your life in a cold, dark watery grave called the Gulf of Mexico.

Flying low was an absolute necessity to avoid detection from the radar that was set up to prevent the penetration of our border. It was called "flying under the radar."

Upon approaching land, flying into a sparsely populated portion of the state was important. It would allow him to come in low. Then by pulling back on the control wheel and pushing down on the throttle, he climbed to a normal height just like any other plane without being noticed. Once over land, completing the journey was as simple as flying over I-10 headed west until he reached his point of destination.

At this point of the trip, he had to focus all of his attention on his plane and stop all distractions. It was time to fly under the radar, because if he was going to get home, he must fly as the "Crow" flies, a feat not many people could do.

Chapter 2

The Beginning

Freddie Wayne Crow was born in Century, Florida, on April 25, 1949. This small impoverished area was located in the northeast corner of Escambia County, the western-most county in the state of Florida.

Escambia is much like the other Florida Panhandle counties where the north end of the county is covered with pine trees and farmland while the south end has the sugary white beaches of the Gulf of Mexico.

The county seat is Pensacola, a Navy town known as the "Cradle of Naval Aviation" and "Home of the Blue Angels." While signs of poverty can be seen throughout the county, it is particularly prominent in Century.

Century came to the Twentieth Century as Teaspoon, a bustling sawmill town full of hope and promise. Then at the turn of the century, Teaspoon changed its name to Century.

When the sawmill closed, the jobs seemed to leave town and have since never returned. Even with such a lack of promise, a sense of pride has always been shared among many of the residents—pride in their town, pride in their high school, and pride in the Century Blackcats, the mascot for their high school sports. Century saw the likes of Nat Showalter (a.k.a. Buck Showalter) of Major League Baseball fame and Anthony Pleasant of National Football League fame grow up and bring pride to the people of Century.

Before Freddie Crow came into this world, there was his oldest sister Bobbie. She was born to Fred and Florence Trussell Crow in Gadsden, Alabama.

At two years of age, Bobbie became the big sister to a new baby brother. Unfortunately, Bobbie's mother experienced complications during childbirth. Realizing she wasn't going to recover from it, Florence called the family to her bedside out of concern for Bobbie's care. Her wish was that Bobbie would be raised by her maternal grandparents so that she could have the influence that comes from a woman's care.

A few days later, Florence succumbed to the complications and died. She was only twenty-two. To exacerbate the tragedy, Bobbie lost her baby brother three days later. She began her life with incredible loss.

Fred continued to farm while in Gadsden, and he spent as much time as possible with Bobbie. After two years, the terrible loss and constant reminders of the area grew too much for him. He went to his in-laws, the Trussells, and informed them that he was going to have to leave. He asked them to go with him. The change of scenery sounded like a good idea, so everyone packed up and headed to Pollard, Alabama.

Pollard is a small town in Escambia County, Alabama, and has been around a long time without much change other than the size of the trees. It can be found about halfway between Flomaton and Brewton. Here, the Trussells ran a small store with living quarters in the back. Fred was able to find work at the Container Mill in Brewton about twenty miles away, to which he commuted daily. This allowed him to see Bobbie in the evenings and maintain a job at the same time.

As solutions were found for difficult situations, Bobbie settled into the life she was given. Things were normal for her, and all was good. Little did she know that it was not to last. The time came when sadness interrupted her life once again. In just a matter of a few years, Bobbie lost both of her grandparents around the same time, both from medical issues. Her world changed once again.

Two aunts were ready and waiting to take care of Bobbie. She ended up living with both, first in Atmore, Alabama, and then in Byrneville, Florida, just a few miles from Century. All of this occurred before she turned eleven years old.

We all reach a time when we can either turn bitter for what has happened to us or be thankful for the blessing of always having our needs met by people who love us. It's a fork in the road and a choice to make, and Bobbie had chosen the latter.

When she was eleven years old, her father Fred met Sybil Nicholas while living in South Flomaton, a small town on the Florida side of Flomaton, Alabama. Incorporated in 1945, it laid between Century and the Florida-Alabama state line. The one-mile stretch made for a tiny dot on the map.

South Flomaton had a City Hall and an unmanned jail. Law enforcement from the area, whether it be deputies, constables, or the city's police chief locked up prisoners and then went back on patrol until there were enough arrestees to make a decent haul to the jail in Pensacola. These transports happened at least daily but sometimes more frequently depending on how full the cells got.

As Fred and Sybil began to spend more time together, it appeared there would soon be a new family. Sybil also brought a child, a son named Hurston, from a previous relationship at an early age. He had been living with his maternal grandparents.

Fred asked Bobbie if she would like to live with him again. She moved in, and soon thereafter, Fred and Sybil got married.

Around this time, Hurston's grandfather died, but he continued to stay with his grandmother in Century. She took on the role of mother, and Hurston called her "Mama" and his mother "Sybil." He visited Sybil often, but as night fell, he wanted to go home and take care of his "mama."

As time went on, Hurston and Bobbie became very close. Bobbie, petite with short brown hair, wasn't allowed to date until she was sixteen, but if Hurston was going somewhere, she was always allowed to accompany him. To Fred, he was a trusted son, a role he deserved.

After two years, Fred and Sybil had their first child together, a beautiful healthy baby girl. Bobbie named her Patricia (Tricia) Ann after a character in a novel she had been reading at the time. Bobbie found taking care of Tricia to be quite easy.

This first child of the blended family was the quiet before the storm because in just fourteen months, along came Freddie Wayne. Bobbie named Freddie as well. "Freddie" for their father Fred and "Wayne" for her favorite movie star at that time, John Wayne.

With two babies in the house, there was never a dull moment. Bobbie soon learned that the quiet times when she was the only child were now gone, and that the responsibilities, the work, the worry, and the joy in raising children had become full-blown.

With her father and stepmother both working, Bobbie was the designated caregiver, and this role began immediately. Changing diapers, feeding babies, and general care were acts of love that came easy to her.

The chase didn't begin until those babies turned two and three. Some days, Bobbie hurried home from school to give the kids a bath, dress them up, and then take them to the goldfish pond at the Flomaton Train Depot. They really seemed to enjoy this excursion, even with the instructions to not get dirty or wet. For Tricia, not getting dirty was a reasonable request that was easy for her to follow. For four-year-old Freddie, though, catching a goldfish while remaining dry or clean was impossible. The desire to hold a goldfish was just too strong, and everyone knows that if you're going to hold a goldfish, you first must catch it—no matter the cost.

During this period, Fred and Sybil spent a great deal of time running their businesses, which were good opportunities for additional income. Crow's Bar, a small store that sold bologna, salt, sugar, or other convenience items, was located next to their house and directly on the Florida-Alabama line. The Crow's Nest was a bar in the Quarters, an African-American part of town that was located not far from where the old sawmill had once operated. Bobbie especially enjoyed this place due to the music and the dancing that took place.

Fred and Sybil relied on Bobbie so much for the care of Tricia and Freddie because of these businesses. Fortunately, Bobbie was not without help. Cookie, an African-American lady hired to cook, clean, and run the house, was there to keep things going. Cookie was the first to feel the brunt of little Freddie Crow.

One of Freddie's earliest pranks was to stand behind the door and call out to Cookie. When she walked through the door, he would jump out from behind it with mischievousness on his face and pee on her leg. Freddie would be admonished for his behavior, but that only lasted until he did it again.

Then there was the matter of bath time. Before Bobbie could go anywhere at night with her friends, her chore was to make sure Freddie and Tricia had a bath. For Tricia, it was a simple task. For little Freddie

Crow, he had to be chased down and put into the tub. On at least three occasions, Freddie used this moment in time to have a bowel movement in the tub. This called for an emptying of water, cleaning of the tub, and a do-over on the bath. All this resulted in Bobbie being late to meet her friends, who invariably wanted to know why.

The admonishments continued as well as the pranks. Bobbie did everything she could to make sure both Tricia and Freddie grew up with good values. On Sundays, they attended the Flomaton Baptist Church as often as possible. She believed that a good firm belief in biblical principles was important, but as time grew on, she couldn't help but feel a little more condemnation than love coming from the church.

She had grown fond of dancing from watching the patrons at the Crow's Nest, but her church spoke of it as a sin. Having parents who ran a bar didn't help either. For all of her disagreements with the church, Bobbie still developed a love of God and fellow man, which she tried to instill in Freddie and Tricia. Because of her influence and efforts to get her younger siblings to church, they obtained a good solid Christian foundation as children.

During these early years, Freddie developed a friendship with the Simpson brothers, Wayne and Bobby. There were other Simpson children, a rather large family by most standards, but Wayne and Bobby were closest to Freddie's age and lived just three doors down.

The Simpsons were not as fortunate financially as the Crow's, but whatever Freddie had, he was more than happy to share. One of those things was his tricycle, and not only his tricycle but Tricia's as well. This kind gesture of making sure they had a tricycle to ride would later be repaid. When Wayne learned how to ride a bicycle, Wayne's mother took on the task of teaching Freddie how to ride one. This sharing-and-caring type of relationship lasted throughout childhood.

From riding bicycles to hunting and fishing, Freddie and the Simpsons did a lot together. Whether they were shooting BB guns or fishing in a ditch, they always had something to occupy their time.

On one occasion, they set out hooks in one of the nearby gravel lakes. Upon checking them, they realized they had caught a very large loggerhead turtle. The boys rushed back to get Fred, who came down and dispatched the turtle for a very big pot of turtle soup. It was the time and place in which they lived.

It was during these early years when Freddie began to develop a reputation as the little rascal of South Flomaton and Century. As he made his way through the community, his brown crewcut giving him away, old women sitting on the front porch could be heard saying, "Is that that Crow Boy?" The other would reply, "Sho is. You better watch him. They say they ain't no tellin what he'll do."

Freddie was eleven years old when Bobbie got married to the love of her life—Louis Jean Grattet—born and raised in Syracuse, New York, with two brothers and two sisters. Paper had brought Lou and Bobbie together. He worked in the converting and packing section of the St. Regis Mill in Cantonment, and Bobbie worked in manufacturing ink for the printing company Sinclair and Valentine. Their meeting for coffee and donuts led to dating and then to marriage. She began her life with Louis in Pensacola and then on to Georgia, away from "her children," but she made weekend trips home to see them.

Around this time, Freddie decided he wanted an alligator. The Crows had a concrete pond at their home, and that would be the perfect place to keep it.

Bobbie and Louis were traveling in South Florida, when they happened upon the opportunity to fulfill Freddie's wish. The baby alligator was purchased at an alligator farm and then carried to Century.

Freddie was now the proud owner of a real alligator. He showed it off to his friends, holding it close to them as he told them it would bite. The baby gator was fed hamburger meat and seemed to be responding very well to it.

As the gator grew, Fred was concerned that it may become too big, so he suggested to Freddie that they take it to the river and let it go. Freddie would hear nothing of it, so the gator remained with the Crow family.

One day, Freddie believed the gator had grown enough that it was time to feed it a steak from the meat department at the store. Unfortunately, the steak proved to be too tough, and the gator choked and died. His death proved to be very difficult on Freddie as he cried for days over his loss.

Freddie's time in school could also be viewed as difficult. He brought home average grades, but he often viewed school as a road-block for what he really wanted to do, which was hunting and fishing. This desire to run free led to missed classes and then whole days.

Eventually, things caught up with him. The principal, Mr. Showalter (Buck Showalter's father), called Fred and asked him to come to the school. Once Fred arrived, Freddie was called to the office.

Fred was the last person Freddie wanted to see there. It didn't take a genius to know the gig was up.

Mr. Showalter informed Fred of Freddie's lack of attendance in school and announced that something would have to be done. He recommended a week of afterschool suspension, but Fred suggested that Mr. Showalter put Freddie to work picking up trash for a month.

Later on, sports helped keep Freddie in school. He loved to play organized sports like football about as much as he liked to hunt and fish.

For all of his pranks and risks, Freddie remained a very generous and caring person. From sharing his tricycle to collecting various items from his parents' store like tomatoes, potatoes, or something sweet, and giving them away to people in the neighborhood, Freddie loved to share what he had. Having parents who owned a bar and a store allowed him to have more things to give away and share.

One day, Freddie rode his motorcycle to football practice. He knew his friend Wayne was too young to play that year, so he tossed his motorcycle's keys to him and told him to go ride it while he was at practice.

The high school in Century was much like all the other schools in the area. It consisted of grades seven through twelve, but the number of students was still relatively small. Consequently, the student body possessed a familiarity amongst each other that was not usually found in schools of a larger size. Although Freddie went to school with kids several years older than him, he was always an equal opportunity prankster, regardless of the ages of his targets. They often looked upon him as a pest because of his antics, but he was still popular and well-liked.

Freddie and the older kids seemed to have a constant back-and-forth battle between them to see who could tease who the most. One day when Freddie was in the eighth grade, he spotted a couple of his favorite prey, seniors Coy Campbell and James Nelson, so he set out to play a prank on them.

The tide soon turned when Coy and James tackled him. While one held him down, the other tied his shoes together in knot after knot after knot. As hard as Freddie tried, he couldn't manage to free himself. They continued to hold him down and punch him until the bell rang for all of the kids to return to class.

Unable to untie his shoes, Freddie hopped back into the school building and into class only to survive for another opportunity to pester the older kids.

During his middle and high school years, Freddie began to develop an interest in airplanes. He put model planes together and hung them from his ceiling. He read books about planes and bought battery-operated planes to fly. He even developed a talent for drawing planes. This love of planes led to Freddie obtaining a pilot's license at a very early age.

It was along about this time when he developed another interest that was every bit as strong—girls. Now taller with an athletic build, he allowed his flat top crewcut to grow out and started dressing sharper. Some folks said no girl was safe once Freddie Crow turned on the charm.

This interest took Freddie and two of his friends, Ricky Crowley and David Calloway, into the high school attic over the girls' locker room. They then used a knife to poke holes in the ceiling. Even though they couldn't see anything, the girls discovered their attempt in the locker room, and an explosion of screams erupted that could be heard throughout the campus.

The boys escaped the attic, but unfortunately, they had written their names on one of the trusses for prosperity. Realizing this was a big mistake, Ricky and David decided to go back and erase their names. Freddie decided this was a bad idea and didn't go.

Going back there turned out to be a bad idea indeed because Mr. Showalter caught Ricky and David in the attic. Freddie was called into the office as well since his name was found along with those of his co-conspirators', but he denied being there. Since they couldn't prove he had written his name there at that time, or that he wrote it at all, he escaped punishment.

As life often goes, the path that Freddie and Wayne walked soon came to a fork. Wayne took the path that led him to the military and Vietnam War, and Freddie chose another path, one that turned out to be painful for him. He was signed up and ready to enter the military. Just before leaving, though, Freddie decided that it simply wasn't something he wanted to do. To remedy that decision, he grabbed his .22 caliber rifle and drove down a secluded road where he stopped on a bridge. He opened the door of his vehicle and set his foot up on the guardrail and then checked for any oncoming traffic. He then aimed the rifle at his foot and fired the shot that would end his military career.

Immediately, he recognized his action as a huge mistake. The pain was unlike anything he had ever experienced. He felt a searing pain from his toes to the top of his head. Blood began to fill his shoe. As he got back into his vehicle, Freddie wondered how he could have been so stupid as to cause himself this type of pain.

Later, he would look upon this pain as pale in comparison to the regret he felt for having shot himself in the first place. He would grow to see this as one of the biggest mistakes of his life because without a doubt, he felt he could have contributed to his country as a fighter pilot. He could have made a difference.

Chapter 3

Rocky

As the foot began to heal, Freddie began to think about what laid ahead. Only two things were certain about his future—it definitely would not involve serving in the military, but it would involve airplanes.

His love of airplanes continued to grow, and his flying skills were becoming more and more proficient. He crop-dusted for Geloyce Ard and Jimmy Nelson in Jay, Florida, and went on pleasure rides whenever he could. The pleasure rides were made possible through a small plane Fred had purchased for Freddie. Freddie continued to let his hair grow to the point that it had almost reached his shoulders. He wanted to impress one of his new favorite pastimes—girls.

Fred, however, was not impressed. So, a simple deal was struck for the airplane, and it required Freddie to cut his hair. Freddie gave in so that he could take friends for plane rides, another one of his favorite things to do. Once they did, they never went on another ride with him again.

Bobby Simpson was one of those friends. Freddie took Bobby up on a ride that involved buzzing swimmers in the gravel lakes on Old

Flomaton Road and then swooping down on some poker players in the woods, sending everyone scrambling. The next stunt was flying under the gas pipeline on the Escambia River. The pipeline reached the banks of the Escambia River but then formed a high arch over the river to avoid problems of rising water levels during times of high tide or heavy rain so boats could continue to navigate under it.

The pipeline called for periodic maintenance in the form of painting, which required painters to attach to the pipeline and paint as they went. It just so happened to be a maintenance day when Freddie took Bobby on a ride. As the plane pulled up underneath the arch, paint brushes flew in one direction while paint cans flew in the other. All this was bad enough, but cutting the engine and going into a nosedive became the final straw and convinced Bobby once and for all to never get into a plane with Freddie Crow again.

Even with all of the excitement of flying, Freddie had also found other interests. The thrill of hunting had become even more exciting when it involved hunting at night and eluding the game wardens. He liked to drive to Stockton, Alabama, to hunt in the misting rain. Once there, it was as simple as picking the one deer you wanted, shooting it, and then heading home where Fred would come out and dress it.

During this time, Freddie also found he had become very fond of marijuana. He never really cared for drinking, but he did enjoy the buzz from smoking a joint. So, in true Freddie Crow fashion, he found a way to bring excitement to marijuana, and he decided to start selling it.

In August 1970, a huge event was scheduled to occur in the Crow family. Tricia was set to marry Harry Mcelwee. He was an Alabama State Trooper who Freddie really didn't see eye to eye with and was not excited about inviting into the family.

Two weeks before the day of the wedding, Freddie and Harry became embroiled in a knock-down drag-out fistfight that would result in Freddie's absence from the wedding. Tricia, being deeply in love, chose to go the way of her husband. So, she and Freddie went their separate ways. It would take years to recover from this clash of personalities.

With Freddie's new interest in marijuana, he found that the faces of his friends began to change. Bobby Simpson, who earned a degree in education and became a teacher in the Escambia County School District, told Freddie that he couldn't be a part of what he was doing with drugs, so they also separated from each other.

Freddie replied, "That's okay. I don't even know why I'm doing it. I know it's wrong."

Freddie started out small like all other people in the business, but his involvement soon increased. Through a friend of a friend, Freddie connected to a supply source in El Paso, Texas. His enterprise, which started with small baggies of marijuana, had evolved into hundreds of pounds of compressed marijuana bricks that were individually wrapped in the trunk of a car.

With Freddie, everything had to contain a thrill. Even the long trek from Century to El Paso and back, which under normal circumstances was one boring trip, was pumped with adrenalin when made under the threat of capture by law enforcement. If not so much the trip out there, then certainly the trip back.

With all of the extra cash, Freddie was also free to live a more extravagant lifestyle. This provided him with more of an opportunity to give to others and fund those good times of movies and hamburgers for him and his friends. Part of that time was spent in and out of Crow's Bar where he met various individuals, those from around town, and those who would come into town to work in the surrounding oil fields. One of those individuals was Rocky LeBlanc.

Rocky was born Sydney LeBlanc in Mobile, Alabama, and he came to Century to work in the oil fields. He already had a successful career as the number-one salesperson for a major insurance company, until one day he decided there had to be more.

He then decided to change careers and go into construction. He wanted to get a union job, but he had to first purchase their book to join. The problem was, the book didn't come overnight. So, while waiting for the union book to arrive, Rocky sold cars, first in Biloxi, Mississippi, and then in Mobile, Alabama.

Once the book arrived and the union job opened up, Rocky found himself working in the Flomaton and Jay oil fields. Free time was spent in Crow's Bar, where he and Freddie crossed paths.

Freddie was his usual entertaining self who never met a stranger. Rocky was a more reserved individual until he felt his opinion needed to be known, and then the shell broke.

Rocky was a fan of the distilled spirits, which was where he and Freddie differed. But what the two men did have in common was that they both liked weed. However, Rocky was not immediately drawn to the smoke. As a matter of fact, his first four attempts at gaining the high were failures, but on the fifth try, he sat back and said to himself, "So, this is what it's all about." From that point on, it was a desired pastime. Somehow the two men had begun to create a bond.

Rocky's job in the oil fields eventually took him to the Rio Grande Valley located on the southern tip of Texas. While there, Rocky's pastime enjoyment found financial opportunity. He knew that Freddie made money from selling marijuana. Being so close to the Mexican border made him realize he could buy pounds of marijuana for a fraction of what he could divide it up for and sell it. So, Rocky began his new endeavor.

Freddie continued to stay in touch with Rocky as he traveled to El Paso to pick up his load of marijuana. As Rocky's business began to grow, he decided to talk to Freddie about becoming his supplier. After all, it made no sense to both of them for Freddie to drive across the state of Texas, if he could get what he needed from Rocky.

A deal was struck between the two friends. So in November 1975, Freddie drove his white Cadillac to "the Valley" for his first business venture with Rocky. On the way while going through Mississippi, he was run off the road and wrecked his car. He was able to catch a ride the rest of the way.

Rocky had already secured all 215 pounds of marijuana in his 1973 Pontiac, and it was ready for the trip. In addition, He gave Freddie explicit instructions about the checkpoints and why he should go through them in the daytime, which was to operate in the open as much as possible. That way, it didn't look like there was something to hide.

The traffic was also heavier in the daytime, and law enforcement had less time to deal with each vehicle in order to keep the traffic moving. At night, things were much different. The officers could become bored to the point that they looked for something to do. Closely scrutinizing each vehicle provided that occupation of time.

Freddie needed a story that would explain his presence at the checkpoint to avoid any problems. To get home undetected, he would need to dress more appropriately. So, he chose to wear a leisure suit that left him looking like John Travolta from *Saturday Night Fever*.

He also sprayed the interior of the car with Lysol deodorizer in an attempt to cover the smell of 215 pounds of marijuana emanating from the trunk. Then as night began to fall on November 23, 1975, Freddie donned his leisure suit and began to make his way home.

Around nine p.m., Freddie made it to the checkpoint at Sarita, Texas, and things just didn't feel right. He began to think he should have listened to Rocky's advice not to go through the checkpoint at night. As he spoke to the Border Patrol Agent, he could feel the tension in him rise.

Freddie began to sweat in his polyester suit as he became more and more nervous. Then he realized the Lysol spray was not a good idea either. The disinfecting smell emanating out of the vehicle was overpowering. No one sprays that much Lysol in their vehicle! What could he have been thinking?

Next came the question, "Can we look in your trunk?"

Only a guilty man would say no, and he didn't want to appear guilty, so he said yes. By now, Freddie pretty much knew the gig was up. The trunk was opened to reveal the suitcases.

The Border Patrol Agent then requested permission to look into the suitcases, and Freddie gave it. All 215 pounds of marijuana was unveiled in all its glory.

The handcuffs were applied, and at the age of twenty-six, Freddie was off to jail. While on his way, all Freddie could think was, *Well, that didn't turn out right.* How was he going to explain this to Rocky? After all, it was Rocky's car that got impounded.

What was done was done. Freddie now had to have a plan to handle this, and the first step would be notifying Rocky and then getting out of jail.

Freddie used his phone call to contact Rocky and inform him he had been arrested. Rocky assured him he'd get started trying to get him out. Rocky contacted a bondsman to get the bond. He had two reasons to help—Freddie was his friend, and he could not turn his back on someone arrested in his car with his pot. It would be too easy for a person in Freddie's position to start talking to the police. Rocky needed to get him out and take care of this.

With the first two objectives complete, Freddie was out of jail, and Rocky was going with him to see an attorney. Mr. Raul Gonzalez, Attorney at Law, was their first stop. The plan was to start with this one and then see different attorneys to find the best one.

After explaining the circumstances to Mr. Gonzalez, Freddie decided to retain him. Rocky tried to talk him out of it. There was something about Mr. Gonzalez that failed to impress Rocky, but Freddie hired him anyway. Whether it was right or wrong, no one will ever know, but in the end, Freddie was sentenced to four years in federal confinement with two years of supervised release.

Rocky kept checking as to when his seized 1973 Pontiac would be available for bids at the law enforcement auction. He was determined not to let the government have his car. Plus, he had hidden a pistol in it, and he wanted to get it back.

As soon as he saw his car was up for auction, he repurchased it. He climbed inside and felt around. There was his Colt .25 caliber pistol tucked away in the seat right where he had left it. He was relieved that it had somehow eluded the extensive search by law enforcement. It happens.

While Rocky, his vehicle, and pistol were all reunited, it would be years before he would see Freddie again.

Rocky started to secretly store away the proceeds of his marijuana business, all the while continuing to experiment with other drugs. Cocaine became a favorite, and he tried it in all forms, even becoming proficient in cooking crack.

His key was to keep a low profile. Before Freddie's arrest, he had often criticized him for trying to live like a rock star. In his opinion, "Crow," as he liked to call him, was just bringing attention to himself, spending his money out in the open. Whether it be on friends or strippers, it didn't matter.

In 1980, it all ended for Rocky. The price of marijuana had reached a point that a lot of people were losing their life over it. People were being shot up in rip-offs, and no one could be trusted. It was time to get out of the business and time to cut out the drug use as well. For some people, it required rehab and therapy, but for Rocky, it was "just say no." Once he decided to quit, it was over.

Rocky went on to bigger and better things, owning four car lots and even becoming a city councilman for the city of Mobile, Alabama. But through it all, he couldn't help but wonder what would ever happen to Crow.

Chapter 4

The Revolving Door

No one wants to do time in prison, and the amount of difficulty one will experience varies and is determined by the type and location of the facility where the time is served. The seriousness of the crime committed often determines the type, and the location becomes a factor when the time is served at great distances away from the family.

There are two prison systems—federal and state. Cases prosecuted in federal court are sentenced to federal prison, while state prosecutions are sentenced to state prisons. Federal prisons are usually nicer facilities with air-conditioned housing. If one is fortunate enough to obtain minimum security housing, it is considered the country club of prisons with minimal tasks included.

In contrast, the state prisons are usually without air-conditioning, even in the South, and the everyday tasks given are much less desirable. In the federal system, gain time, or time off from a sentence, is offered and automatically given for good behavior. The most anyone can hope to earn is fifty-four days a year with no parole, that is unless the politicians decide they don't want to house nonviolent offenders any longer. In that situation, thousands will be released early. In the state system, before the Truth in Sentencing Act of 1983, serving only half a sentence was not uncommon, depending on overcrowding and budgets.

Freddie was sentenced to four years federal prison, which amounts to three years and five months. This time was served at the Eglin Facility located in Okaloosa County in the Florida Panhandle. This facility is often reserved for the white-collar criminals who were unable to avoid arrest and conviction.

Freddie was fortunate to be placed in this facility with close proximity to family and friends but also with a more laid-back approach to doing time. While each inmate was given tasks to perform, they weren't digging ditches. Chores included laundry and house cleaning, but every prison needs a cook, and that was right down Freddie's alley. In fact, Freddie eventually earned the name "Freddie Crocker" for his love of cooking. As fortunate as he was, though, at the end of the day, he was still in prison, which meant he couldn't go home.

His time went by without incident. Upon completion of his allotted sentence, he was released to serve two years of supervised release, which was much the same as state probation. The inmate was required to report to a controlling officer, who determined how often the checking in took place as well as assured certain guidelines were kept. The inmate also had to acquire some type of approved employment, undergo drug screening, and display an ability to stay out of trouble. Freddie did well with all but the last one—he resumed his marijuana selling activities.

Even though Freddie gained his release from prison in 1979, it turned out to be a difficult year. To begin with, Freddie's mother Sybil made a decision to ask Fred for a divorce. She and Fred loved to fish as a pastime but not together. So, Sybil started fishing with Buddy Merritt and started developing feelings for him. She made the announcement to Fred at home.

The news broke Fred's heart, which sent Freddie into a rage. He quickly declared that his mother was not going anywhere. He then picked up a rifle, went outside, and proceeded to shoot out all four tires on Sybil's vehicle.

Bobbie later asked Freddie why he would do such a thing, and Freddie replied, "I just felt like shooting something, and I thought that was a good place to start." The flat tires did not keep Sybil from leaving, and the divorce was obtained.

The events didn't improve. On April, 9, 1979, Freddie found himself speeding through the streets of Pensacola, when all of the sudden, blue lights appeared in his rearview mirror. Normally, this would not be cause for panic. However, when you're carrying two bags of marijuana, each with the quantity large enough to be considered for distribution, and you've just been released from prison while still under supervised release, the fight or flight instinct kicks in. Freddie didn't want to fight, so the chase was on. As the old saying goes, you might be able to outrun the police car, but you can't outrun the police radio.

Additional units joined in the chase, so Freddie was soon corralled, and the chase was over. He was placed under arrest for two counts of possession of marijuana over five grams, possession with intent to distribute, attempt to elude, and willful and wanton reckless driving. These were all state charges; however, the part of supervised release concerning his displaying an ability to stay out of trouble generated a federal charge for violation probation.

For Freddie's romp in Pensacola, he was convicted of reckless driving and received thirty days in the county jail. The other state charges were dropped, happily returning him to the federal authorities for the violation of supervised release.

Once the thirty days were served, the U.S. Marshals picked him up where he eventually ended up in the Federal Corrections Institute in Tallahassee, Florida, to serve the remainder of his probation.

Freddie arrived in Tallahassee to begin his sentence. The usual procedures were conducted: intake interviews, job assignments, and issuing of a bedroll. He would begin his second federal incarceration, which would not end until March 1980.

ENTER EDWARD HUDSON

In June of 1980, a fresh young face just out of college appeared at the Century Police Department. The city of South Flomaton had taken on the name of Century in 1979, and then voted to annex in the unincorporated section of Century on April 22, 1980. It was in need of another police officer.

Edward Hudson, ten years junior to Freddie Crow, had grown up in the north central part of Escambia County in a small rural community called Walnut Hill. The heart of Walnut Hill consisted of two general stores with gas pumps and Ernest Ward School, the home of the Golden Eagles. First-through twelfth grade all studied under one roof. The football stadium was made from concrete slabs. Basketball games were played in an old airplane hangar that had been converted to a gym, and baseball had to be played in the daytime because there were no floodlights.

The community was proud of its Walnut Hill Grain Elevator, the largest structure for as far as the eye could see. Farmers would travel for miles to bring and store their grain until it could be sold.

Edward grew up working on farms doing various chores that often turned into very long days, but the toting of brick and block and making mortar for his father's masonry business was what convinced him to go to college. If the masonry business sent Edward to college, it was the other part of his upbringing that gave him direction. The Sunday mornings, Sunday nights, Wednesday nights, and every night during revival at the Oak Grove Baptist Church was where Edward came to understand the sacrifice given by Jesus Christ as well as where he was given the heart of a servant.

Upon graduating high school in 1976, Edward knew he wanted a service-oriented job. No wars were being fought. In that particular time, there wasn't even a way to sign up for the draft, so the logical alternative was to go into law enforcement.

Since getting a job in law enforcement at seventeen years of age was impossible, college seemed to be the route to go. During the four years of college where he majored in law enforcement and subsequently, criminal justice administration, the instructors insisted on calling him "Ed." So from then on, outside of family and those close in the community, Edward became Ed.

His oldest brother Paul was a police officer for the city of Flomaton. Working close to him just seemed like a good idea. Ed's dream job was to patrol the roads of North Escambia County, but the Escambia County Sheriff's Department wasn't hiring at the time, and the Century Police Department provided valuable experience. Upon starting his new job as a police officer, he stood at five foot ten with just enough weight to pack a punch. Realizing he seemed to wear the same face he did as a toddler, he sported a brown mustache in an effort to look older and more mature.

Chief John McLain showed Ed the ropes. There weren't a lot of ropes to show in a five-man department, though. They had a Ford

LTD II for a patrol car that had a radio on which you talked to the dispatchers. Other than that, the time had come to go learn the streets, which also didn't take long in a city three miles long and one mile wide.

Just before Ed hit those mean streets of Century, the chief asked if he was familiar with Jesse McGraw. He was. They had grown up together in the Walnut Hill area. Jesse was two years older than Ed, but at Ernest Ward, you knew everyone, and everyone knew you.

Jesse was notorious for how he seemed to live to pick on people. He took great delight in giving someone a pop on the head that hurt. If their feet were kicked out from under them while walking down the hall, Jesse was probably the one who did it.

Yes, Ed Hudson was very familiar with Jesse McGraw. The chief explained that Jesse had a warrant for a bad check and if Ed saw him, he was to pick him up.

On one of the few occasions Ed worked the day shift, he began his rounds around ten o'clock that early summer morning with weather typical for this part of the country. It emanated just enough heat and breeze to let one know that spring was gone, and the scorching days of July and August had yet to arrive.

The city was easy enough to learn—Highway 29 ran north and south with a few streets on each side and most of the businesses on the most northern end. Ed needed to check the bars, which opened around nine in the morning. It didn't take a lot of experience to recognize that a bar could be a location for trouble, so he decided to go ahead and get acquainted with them. The Melody Lounge on the south end of town was primarily an African-American bar while Odom's Bar and Crow's Bar on the north end were mixed, sort of.

Twenty years after desegregation, both Odom's and Crow's still had two sections. The front sections were for all intents and purposes Caucasian. The back sections were for the African Americans.

A rather noticeable difference was also in the amenities of both bars. The front sections had a nice bar, jukebox, and pool tables. The back sections had a bench. Steadfast rules of segregation were not enforced, and no one ever seemed to complain. Everyone just seemed happy to have a place to go. An air of apathy in the Deep South on the part of both races didn't seem to be reflective of the overall progression toward racial equality in the 1980s.

Crow's Bar was the first stop. Ed walked in and stopped to let his eyes adjust to the lighting. The first thing he noticed was the wire cage built around the jukebox, a form of protection for those rowdy times when pool cues and bar stools where thrown around.

Then there was the bar where a couple of midday drinkers were already seeking the cure to their problems at the bottom of the glass. One of them happened to be none other than Jesse McGraw. He might have aged a little, but he still had that same curly blonde hair.

Ed walked up to him, and for a brief time, they held a reunion. The two men talked about school and the jobs Jesse had since high school. He also told Ed about the troubles that came from a bad marriage.

Then the bad news was delivered to Jesse along with the handcuffs. He offered no resistance, no back talk. He seemed sad as though the last bad thing that could happen to him had just happened, and tears rolled down his face. Jesse was broken.

The first of many trips into Crow's Bar gave Ed his first arrest and would become a familiar place with a familiar name—Freddie Crow. At that time, Ed had never heard of Freddie Crow. Within a few short months, though, he would not only learn of Freddie Crow the drug smuggler, but also of Freddie Crow the pilot.

Numerous stories circulated about Freddie, but the one that stuck in Ed's mind was how he had flown a plane under the bridge on Highway 4 going to Jay. Ed just knew he had to be crazy.

Ed continued to work at the Century P.D. until September 1981, when he was hired for his dream job—working for the Escambia County Sheriff's Department. He was assigned to patrol the north end of the county. It would take nine years before Ed and Freddie would finally meet face to face.

After his release in March 1980, Freddie managed to stay out of trouble for a while. That was when the long-time feud between Freddie and his Alabama State Trooper brother-in-law Harry came to a head.

In December 1981, Harry made contact with Corporal Rhett Smith of the Escambia County Sheriff's Office in Pensacola. He informed Corporal Smith of marijuana plants drying in the barn behind Fred Crow's residence on Freedom Road in Century. Harry explained that the plants actually belonged to Fred's son, Freddie.

A quick glance of Freddie's criminal history, and considering Harry's position with the Alabama State Troopers, it was an easy search warrant to write for Corporal Smith.

The next night, the Escambia County Narcotics Unit arrived at the home of Fred Crow where they proceeded to search the barn and residence for illegal drugs. Fred was home along with a visitor, Timothy "Timbo" Campbell.

Timbo stood about six foot with a lean build and brown hair. He had been close friends with Freddie and Fred for years. He was the son of James Campbell, who many described as good a man as you could find. Mr. James, as many called him, was the owner of Campbell's Sand and Gravel in Century. Freddie had known Mr. James from his youth and looked up to him immensely. By most standards, he was a wealthy man, but he raised a troubled son. Timbo could be a very friendly person, but he had a mean streak and a passion for excitement that caused him to choose the wrong road.

At first, the narcotics team believed Timbo to be Freddie, so they searched and handcuffed him. But that was quickly corrected when they read Timbo's ID and realized their mistake, so they removed the handcuffs. The search revealed the drying marijuana plants along with a bonus—the discovery of enough cocaine to charge with intent to distribute.

With Freddie working in Donalsonville, Georgia, as a crop-duster (with a side job of drug smuggling), Fred denied any knowledge of the drugs. Of course, no one ever came right out and said whether or not Fred actually knew about the drugs, but it was in his barn. Regardless, the narcotics squad had been working with information that said it belonged to Freddie.

Freddie stayed in Georgia for the next two months, hoping the charges would go away. They didn't, so he finally came back to Escambia County to answer to them. He pleaded guilty to the charge of possession of cocaine and received a five-year sentence in state prison.

Freddie later said that there was no way he could have let his dad go to prison, leading one to wonder if the drugs actually did belong to Fred. The other question was whether Harry acted out of a sense of duty or from a deep-rooted dislike of Freddie. Only Harry could answer that question, but he never talked about it to anyone.

The state prison system is similar yet different from the federal prison system. All inmates must first enter through a reception center. Here, the inmate is classified and screened to determine the prison best suited for the inmate to do his sentence based on the crime and proximity to family. Until that determination is made, they stay at the reception center.

Phone calls are limited, and there are no vocational or educational programs. Special visits can be arranged.

Freddie's oldest sister Bobbie visited him during this time, something she tried to do on a regular basis. While she could never condone his illegal activity, she just couldn't turn her back on him either, even if it did call for uncomfortable situations.

One such visit required Bobbie to submit to a pat-down search. This was something she had never experienced in a federal prison. Just the thought was horrifying, but the actual event left her without words. She could feel the blood rise to her head throughout the process. By the time she made it to where Freddie was, she was fit to be tied.

The first thing she could think to say was, "Freddie, they strip searched me!"

Freddie sat back, and a big grin spread across his face. "Wasn't that fun!"

Bobbie glanced around and then leaned forward, replying with a snarl. "*No!*"

Of course, Freddie couldn't leave it alone, so he had to ask, "Didn't it feel good?"

Bobbie realized the term "strip search" might not be the right words to describe the pat-down she experienced. She wasn't exactly sure why she called it that because no clothing was removed. They just seemed to fit the way she felt.

Freddie eventually ended up at the Berrydale Road Camp in Santa Rosa County just down the road from Century. The Road Camp was a welcome relief from the hardcore inmates of the more confining institutions. Visits were easier for family and friends, and Bobbie didn't have to submit to any more "strip searches." Good friends like Jimmy

Earl and Rita Crowley, along with other friends and family members, were faithful to come and see Freddie.

While there, he received one of the biggest surprises in the way of a visit. The guards came to him and told him to prepare for a special visit, but they didn't tell him who it was.

Before long, the yard was cleared, and only Freddie and the picnic tables were left. The first clue came when Freddie recognized the big tour bus that pulled up to the camp's property. Shortly thereafter, a mountain of a man with long hair and a beard stepped off that bus. His name was William Lee Golden.

William Lee Golden was born to a peanut and cotton farmer in Dixonville, Alabama, a small farming community south of Brewton, Alabama, on the Florida-Alabama line. William grew up working on the farm, but his interest rested in music.

It took a while for a boy in Dixonville, Alabama, to make it in the music business. In the meantime, Crow's Bar became a hangout for William, and he developed a special relationship with Fred that extended to his son in later years.

In 1965, William finally made it big and became a member of the Oak Ridge Boys. This singing quartet formed in the early forties and became a well-respected gospel group that would later produce numerous country hits. Even after making it big, William would still return to Century to see Fred. They had the kind of friendship that brought them to share Christmas dinners together at Fred's home.

That friendship also brought William to Berrydale Road Camp. The yard's gates were opened, and William sauntered in like he owned the place.

He and Freddie sat down at one of the round picnic tables and began to talk. Before long, William reached into his jacket pocket and pulled out a marijuana joint.

Freddie's eyes were as big as saucers. "Are you trying to get locked up in here with me?" he asked William.

William replied in his deep baritone voice, "It'll be all right."

So, the two of them sat in the yard at the picnic table and talked while smoking a joint.

The one group of visitors Freddie could have done without while serving this sentence was the U.S. Marshalls. They came to re-arrest him on September 12, 1982, for another charge, which was a federal offense. His activities before these Escambia County charges had finally caught up with him. They consisted of conspiracy to traffic in cannabis and trafficking in cannabis, which were charges filed for a case in Wauchula, Hardee County, Florida, about seventy miles outside of Tampa.

While living in Georgia, Freddie had been flying for a group of people in Tampa who brought in loads of marijuana. One particular offload site turned out to be similar to a dyke holding back water. Upon landing, the ground was wet, bogging down the wheels and causing the nose of the plane to dive into the mud. Freddie escaped without injury.

The ground crew unloaded the airplane. As they were about to leave, Freddie suggested they burn the plane to destroy evidence, but it wasn't done. The plane was later discovered by law enforcement. With a little crime scene work and investigation, the residue left on the plane provided a basis for a trafficking charge.

These federal charges carried a five-year sentence to run concurrent with the five-year state sentence Freddie was already serving. A concurrent sentence is when two or more sentences are served at the same time as opposed to a consecutive sentence, which are served separately.

This being the case, Freddie finished his sentence in federal prison, since the federal charge trumped the state charges. He was brought back to the Federal Correctional Institute (F.C.I.) in Tallahassee, Florida, for conspiracy to traffic in marijuana and trafficking in marijuana. This time, he would meet a very interesting person.

Chapter 5

Dekle

For Freddie, coming back to F.C.I. Tallahassee wasn't quite like coming home, but it did have a familiar feel to it. The process was much the same—bedrolls handed out and assignments given. He was then taken to his designated cell that he would share with another inmate.

There was always apprehension about just how well he would get along with the other inmates. That apprehension was quickly calmed when he walked into his cell to see a man on his bunk reading an airplane magazine.

Freddie's new cellmate was Billy Dekle. Some folks say that people are brought together by fate. There are also those who say that prison is a training ground and network for criminals. Whether it was one or both, Freddie and Billy quickly bonded over their mutual love of flying.

William ("Billy") Ervin Dekle was born in Gainesville, Florida, the same year as Freddie. Billy's great-grandfather was a Bradford County Judge, and his grandfather was a Union County Sheriff who also retired from the Florida Department of Corrections. He then went on to become the Mayor of Lake Butler.

Donald Dekle, Billy's father, worked in the Florida Department of Corrections where he rose to the rank of major. His mother Jewel became a school teacher in Lake City where Billy grew up on a farm with his sister Lucy and brother George.

Lucy decided to follow in the family footsteps and work for the Florida Department of Corrections at Lake Butler. George went to law school and later became employed as an Assistant State Attorney. While all of the Dekles were accomplished in their field, George Robert (Bob) Dekle was probably the one who possessed the most notoriety.

Bob used his country upbringing in court proceedings to play up the hayseed plowboy persona while all the time planning a brilliant strategy. He used "tricks" like bringing a clear plastic cup to a deposition to spit his tobacco juice in and then set on the table. This did more than make him look country; it distracted those in the room to the point of nausea.

Another point of distraction in a deposition was taking his notes in Greek miniscule script. Attorneys would strain to make out what he was writing. On one occasion, Bob turned his notebook around to the attorney and said, "Here, take a closer look." Bob Dekle was an accomplished attorney, but it was the prosecution of Ted Bundy that would bring out the best in him.

Ted Bundy was a notorious serial killer who would later confess to thirty homicides. However, it was the murder of twelve-year-old Kimberly Leach, which Bob Dekle prosecuted, and Bundy's subsequent capture in Pensacola that would lead Ted Bundy to the electric chair on January 24, 1989.

The Dekles were a family who served the state of Florida well, except for Billy. In 1979, Billy Dekle was arrested by the Kingston,

Jamaica Police Department. He was the pilot of a plane that had been loaded with several hundred pounds of marijuana, or ganja as they refer to it on the island. The Kingston Police swooped down upon the unsuspecting smugglers as Dekle attempted to take flight. Unfortunately, the plane had been loaded to a capacity, which slowed it to a point that take off was thwarted by the oncoming police. For all this effort, Dekle served thirty days in the Jamaican jail.

Dekle went on to have several run-ins with the law, but he always seemed to put off capture, at least for a while. Flying loads of marijuana into the country required an organization compiled of people abroad and at home. The more people involved, the more likely someone would slip up and get arrested. As the members of one organization begin to get knocked off, another organization needed to be started. This was where conspiracies begin, and the conspiracy charge was the prosecutor's best friend.

A conspiracy charge is used when two or more people come to a mutual agreement to commit a crime. For the purposes of making the charge of conspiracy, the clock begins at that point the agreement to commit the crime occurs. As people are brought into the operation, they also become involved in the conspiracy. This is where it gets confusing. A person who enters the conspiracy in the beginning is responsible for everything the organization does until arrest, even if this person elects to walk away from the organization at some point. A person who enters the conspiracy later on is only responsible from the time he enters until arrest. The theory is, the person who enters the conspiracy in the beginning has enabled the organization to exist. The person who enters the conspiracy later on has forwarded the conspiracy and allowed it to continue. This timeline becomes important when the prosecution begins to add up the number and pounds of each load.

These dates also became a problem for Dekle as he eluded arrest, and his organization began to be picked off by law enforcement. It was imperative that Dekle get a new organization so that he could continue bringing in loads.

This new organization created a new conspiracy. Eventually, Dekle was captured for the first conspiracy, and while he sat in jail, the case was being made for the second conspiracy. He had nothing left to do but get out of jail, get a new crew, and go again. He had to make a living, so the only thing he could do was what he knew how to do—covert smuggling.

One could argue that the Dekle-Crow conspiracy began in F.C.I. Tallahassee, or at least that's where Freddie joined in. Of course, they had to first get to know one another and build trust. As they began to share their experiences, a bond seemed to grow between the two men.

Freddie and Dekle spent a lot of time talking about Dekle's organization and who did what in each smuggling venture. By all accounts, Dekle was well-connected in the smuggling business. For instance, he knew Glen Monroe from many previous smuggling operations. And then Monroe had connections with Johnny Crawford, who was a marijuana supply source in Belize. Freddie was eager to become a part of this organization. He just needed to finish up his prison term.

Dekle gained his freedom in February, 1986, and Freddie followed suit. He took wing, so to speak, and got released in August of the same year. Freddie was the type to keep in touch and was ready to get back to the life of smuggling. So, in December 1986, all of the connections began to come together.

Glen Monroe was in charge of organizing the loads, which was something he had become quite good at doing. He had already been involved with approximately 100 loads, and more importantly, he had organized at least forty of them. Up until this point, he had never lost a load, but this was not to say he didn't have bad luck.

One such incident occurred on January 21, 1986, while Dekle and Freddie were still in prison. Monroe had organized a load that was being flown into an agreed-upon open field surrounded by tall pine trees in Escambia County, Alabama. The plane was able to fly low enough during several passes so that the marijuana bales could be kicked out of it without being noticed. It was a way to bring in a load when an airstrip wasn't available.

However, they didn't know about the hunter nearby. He notified the authorities, but not before the ground crew could pick up all but one bale and leave the area.

Deputy Claude Cosey from Alabama's Escambia County Sheriff's Department arrived to find a forty-five-pound bale hanging in a pine tree caught up in thick vines. He and Chief Deputy Stan Stewart pulled the bale down just to make sure of what they were looking at. A small portion of the bale wrap was peeled back to see that it was marijuana. The deputies then attempted to put the bale back in the tree.

That night, one of the coldest of the year, Deputy Cosey and Chief Deputy Stewart set up surveillance in the woods along the tree line. Four men carrying long guns walked into the field and then to where the bale was. Their flashlights shone up on the bale still hanging in the tree. The deputies could hear conversation taking place, but they couldn't make out what was said.

Not long afterward, the men walked away, leaving the bale behind. It's not known if witnessing the men approach the bale and conversing about it could be considered suspicious or just why they left it behind. However, without them taking possession of it, Chief Deputy Stewart made the decision not to make contact with them. Deputy Causey just wanted to get warm because he thought he was going to freeze to death.

Consequently, Glen Monroe was able to continue with his livelihood another day. He was not one to confine his methods of operation. He had access to a sailboat, and sailboats could carry a lot of marijuana.

Such was the case in July 1986, when 4,600 pounds of marijuana were arriving near Morehead City, North Carolina. Monroe put together a ground crew to offload the cargo. This operation could eventually be seen as the beginning of the end for Glen Monroe. One of the ground crew, Brent Gibbs, was arrested by North Carolina authorities at the scene. While the rest of the crew escaped, the dominos began to fall.

As the saying goes, the show must go on. So, in December 1986, Monroe and Dekle agreed to bring in a load to Suwannee County. Monroe picked the ground crew, which consisted of Bruce Wilson, Sr., James McDonald, and Buddy "Indian" Davis, all associates of Monroe.

Dekle hired Freddie to copilot a Piper Navajo, a twin-engine airplane with a larger passenger compartment than the single-engine Cessna. More power and more storage meant larger loads. Together, the two flew to Belize and brought back 1,200 pounds of marijuana to a secluded strip of ground in Suwanee County suitable to land a plane, but maybe not secluded enough.

Donald Bossuyt was a farmer there. He knew the area, and he knew what should and shouldn't be going on there. Planes landing on the backside of fields with men unloading bundles was definitely not on the list of things that should be going on. Bossuyt felt a quick call to the Suwannee County Sheriff's Department was in order.

Of course, no one involved in this operation knew about Bossuyt watching them, so they continued with their plan. Fortunately, the plane landed without incident.

When the doors opened, the copilot, whom they had not yet seen, stepped out of the plane dressed in camo fatigues, a scalper knife in a knife sheath on his side, and camo paint completely covering his face. No one in the offload crew had a clue of what or who that was.

Freddie had told Dekle he didn't want to be recognized, and this was his way of trying to save some anonymity. This disguise allowed Freddie to go undetected for years because all anyone had known him by was the name the organization had given him—Rambo.

The 1,200 pounds of marijuana were loaded onto vehicles with 950 of those pounds being loaded onto Monroe's pickup truck. So as not to leave behind evidence of smuggling, Dekle ripped the collapsible fuel tank out of the plane's cargo area and left it at the offload site as they took off in their vehicles.

Monroe, still puzzled by this new Rambo character, began to make his way to the road. All of the sudden, he realized he had a flat tire. He abandoned the truck with the 950 pounds of marijuana, and just like that, Monroe had lost his first load. Now the Suwannee County Sheriff's Department would have a truck loaded with marijuana and a bladder tank for evidence.

Bruce Gibbs had been feeling the heat from his brother Brent Gibbs's 1986 arrest in North Carolina. So, by early 1987, he finally came out of hiding from the disastrous sailboat load and was ready to smuggle again. This load was planned in great detail. They didn't need any mistakes because of the 950 pounds that was lost.

Dekle stole a six-passenger single-engine Cessna 210 in Lake City. It had retractable landing gear and wings that spanned across the top of the cabin. This new asset would cut down on the cost of having to pay someone to use their plane. Gibbs surveyed a landing site in Liberty County in Florida, and Dekle approved it.

Assignments were given to the ground crew. Gibbs would serve as security, looking for law enforcement or anyone else coming close. Monroe and one of the ground crew, Richard King, were together in Monroe's truck. Both Monroe and King would assist with the offload, and King would also serve as a lookout. Furthermore, the two men provided an additional vehicle in case something went wrong, like another flat tire.

Bruce Gibbs recruited two of his friends, Hal Walker and Brian Cowart, to assist in the offload and to drive his truck. Dekle hired Freddie to pilot the plane to make the flight.

When the plane landed at dusk, the load was put onto Gibb's truck, and everything went according to plan. The plane was left on the Liberty County dirt road, and the marijuana was taken to a stash house. The next day, it was weighed and loaded into vehicles for the buyer, Mack Lewis, to take back to Tennessee.

Monroe paid Hal Walker and Brian Cowart $15,000 each and allowed them to sell 250 pounds of the marijuana, after which they would pay Monroe $137,500 once it was sold. The money was then divided up between Bruce Gibbs, Glen Monroe, and Billy Dekle. Freddie received the regular pilot's pay of $40,000.

In May, 1987, plans were made for another load. Bruce Gibbs met with Glen Monroe, offloader and lookout Richard King, and Robert Crawford to discuss the next venture. Robert Crawford, no relation to Belize supplier Johnny Crawford, was another smuggler interested in helping finance the load and receiving a portion of the proceeds. Gibbs and Monroe discussed the site of Compass Lake, just north of Panama City.

Everything was a go, but the next domino fell. Glen Monroe's past had finally caught up to him. He had been a fugitive for a while, but then he was arrested in Orlando, Florida, on smuggling charges.

One would think that lessons would be learned here, but it just wasn't the case. Ground crew member Bruce Wilson, Sr., met with Billy Dekle, and they decided to go ahead with the load anyway.

So, in June 1987, Dekle and Freddie flew financer Robert Crawford's Piper Aztec to Belize. The Piper Aztec, like the Navajo, was a twin-engine plane with the wings mounted on the lower side of the cabin. It was considered a workhorse where the Navajo was more of a family cruiser.

Once again, the aircraft was loaded with 900 pounds of marijuana purchased from Belize supplier Johnny Crawford. While this was going on, Gibbs was getting his ground crew ready. Bruce Gibbs and Richard King took care of security. They used two-way radios to contact the plane upon approach to advise if the sight was clear for landing.

Ground crew member Bruce Wilson Sr., and Jr., worked together, as all fathers and sons should do, to load marijuana into their truck. Willard Nunnally, who was brought on to take Monroe's place, picked up Dekle and loaded the additional marijuana into his truck. Freddie took the plane back to Lake City.

Everything went according to plan. The marijuana was taken to a stash house owned by Walter Mark Chitty. The next day, Robert Crawford and buyer Mack Lewis took control of the marijuana. Lewis brought his portion back to Tennessee. Even though Monroe was incarcerated at the time, Dekle still paid him $10,000 just because he thought he could use it.

This turned out to be the last load for Bruce Gibbs. As the sailboat case began to pull more people into it, Gibbs felt it would be best to lay low; however, in January 1988, it was time for Gibbs to pay for his transgressions. He was arrested in his hometown of Enterprise, Alabama.

Gibbs would be missed. Not only was he dependable at putting ground crews together and finding locations to offload, but he was also a master forger. He was the one who kept everyone in their fake identifications. Whether they were used for those with pending indictments or just a means to mask activity, such as hotel rentals or buying commercial airline tickets, a good set of fake I.D.s were in high demand. Yes, he would certainly be missed.

In July 1987, Robert Crawford was ready to finance another load. Dekle and Bruce Wilson Sr., once again identified the offload site. Dekle hired Freddie to fly Robert Crawford's Cessna 206 to Belize where another load would be purchased from Johnny Crawford.

Freddie obtained 600 pounds of marijuana and flew back to the Santa Rosa offload site in Mclellen, just south of the Alabama-Florida state line. The ground crew of Dekle, Bruce Wilson Sr., and James McDonald were waiting as Freddie landed the plane. Once the plane stopped, Rambo exited the plane, and the marijuana was loaded into the two transport vehicles.

McDonald then flew the now-empty plane to Tallahassee while Dekle took the marijuana to a stash house nearby. The next morning, Billy Dekle and Bruce Wilson Sr., weighed the marijuana and then transported it to Century, Florida, where it was delivered to Robert Crawford's people.

Wilson Sr., went on to bring in additional loads with his own pilots, but Dekle had other plans. He had decided to go with a new partner and crew. Things were about to change for Freddie, not only in the smuggling business, but in his personal life as well.

Chapter 6

New Partnerships

Sometime prior to September 1987, Billy Dekle and Freddie discussed putting their own load together. Freddie knew people he could call on to help. It wouldn't really be that different from what they had been doing, except they could keep more of the profits for themselves. Dekle purchased his own plane, a Cessna 210, so this would be a very easy business startup, or so it seemed.

In September 1987, Dekle took off in his newly purchased airplane, and the ground crew made up of Freddie and Timbo Campbell were ready to offload. Then Freddie received a page from Dekle telling him that he had landed in Belize. He advised Freddie to be at a certain payphone at a certain time.

It was the way they communicated. Payphones were much harder for law enforcement to monitor, but even then, the need to talk in code was an extra precaution.

When Freddie and Dekle finally made contact, Dekle informed Freddie that he had wrecked the truck. Normally when you're in the business of airplanes, the wrecking of a truck is a minor inconvenience.

But when you're running a clandestine smuggling operation and you have to talk in code, you know truck means airplane.

It takes a good pilot to survive a crash landing—good and lucky. As Dekle landed his plane on the Belize strip, the nose gear of the plane broke, rendering the plane useless and shaking up the unshakeable Billy Dekle. "However," as they say in pilot circles, "any landing you can walk away from is a good landing." Dekle walked away to find a phone to call and report the mishap to Freddie.

Freddie went to work to take care of the problem. He contacted Bruce Wilson Sr., and secured the use of his Aztec to fly to Belize. Then it was just a matter of flying to Belize and picking up the load and Dekle. Quick thinking and coming to the rescue certainly proved Freddie's value as a partner.

The 700 pounds of marijuana were flown into a strip owned by a farmer—Joe Jones of Jay, Florida. Freddie had known him over the years and had felt comfortable enough to approach him about using his strip. Jones agreed.

Timbo was there waiting to offload, which went off without a hitch. Of the 700 pounds, 200 were sold to a distributor, Randy Cannon of Troy, Alabama, while the rest was distributed to other people in smaller quantities.

In January 1988, Dekle purchased another airplane, this time his own Aztec. Needing to have it checked out before making a trip, Dekle flew northwest of Atmore, Alabama, and into an FBO (Fixed Base Operation), a strip where aircraft are operated for various reasons.

This particular FBO was used primarily for crop-dusting and was operated by Blayne Camp, an acquaintance from Freddie's crop-dusting days. Camp was also called to repair airplanes.

Over the course of 1988, Camp worked on airplanes four or five times for Freddie and Dekle, doing electrical work, installing a loran (navigational instrument), and installing auxiliary fuel tanks. These tanks were added to the wing tips and could possibly extend the flight time by 170 miles, something that came in handy when flying to and from Belize.

Camp also gave opinions to Dekle (and later a jury), and in his opinion, the Aztec was a piece of junk that he was afraid someone would get hurt in. For Camp's services, over the course of a year, he received $13,900 cash.

In spite of Camp's warnings, the next load was planned with the Aztec. In February 1988, Freddie and Dekle flew the Aztec to Belize where once again, a load of 800 pounds of marijuana was purchased from Johnny Crawford. The plane returned to the familiar McLellan strip where Timbo and Joe Jones offloaded the cargo. John Cochran, Randy Cannon, and Indian distributed it. After this load, the worn-out Aztec was traded for a Cessna 210, and the smuggling continued.

While business was booming and things were going good, Freddie began to turn his attention in another direction. He liked to eat at a restaurant in Destin, and it had a cute little red head there he liked to have wait on him.

Her name was Kathy Salter. She might just be the one who could pull Freddie away from all the other girls in the bars and strip clubs. There was just something about her that caused him to go to Bobbie and have her press his shirts because the dry cleaners didn't do a good enough job. She was the kind of girl who made him request Maine lobsters be flown in from Maine and delivered to a restaurant in Destin for a special dinner. Yes, Freddie was smitten.

Not long afterward, Kathy moved into the Crow household on Freeman Road in Century. Freddie had been living there alone with Fred for the last nine years since his mother had moved out. Unfortunately, she and Fred's marriage didn't stand the test of time.

Kathy started to feel at home immediately, like it was indeed *her* home. The Freeman Road residence was one of the nicer places in Century. The brick columns, which proudly stood at the property's entrance, led to a long winding concrete driveway that passed by a fish pond, neatly trimmed hedges, the large rock-masonry A-frame house, and eventually to a concrete pad at the rear that housed a barn and showed off a swimming pool. The front center of the house was all glass and single-story wings protruded on each side. Space was not the problem.

Fred had kind of liked his and Freddie's arrangement, so he was not particularly fond of Kathy coming in and taking over. She, on the other hand, was not there to please Fred. Freddie attempted to be the peacemaker, but the time came when he didn't have to worry about that anymore.

Fred Crow was not in the best of health. He had open-heart surgery a few years earlier. The doctors said he had an excellent recovery. He did fine for a while, but then the pains in the stomach came and increased until Fred went to the doctor in November 1988, and learned he had had an abdominal aneurism, which required surgery very soon.

The doctors sent him home to enjoy Thanksgiving, and Bobbie was there to try to see that he did. She took him out to the country store in Byrneville where Fred loved to go for conversation. While he was there, he purchased the forbidden prize he so much enjoyed—a MoonPie™. The look in his eye, however, gave a hint of bad things to come. It was as though Fred knew he was at his end.

On December 2, 1988, Fred underwent surgery and ultimately succumbed to his condition. The loss was hard for those who knew him, especially his family.

In fact, the loss of a loved one can cause stress and depression, but add a volatile relationship to it, and there's bound to be an escalation of these problems. As time progressed, what seemed to be a fine mixture of personalities between Kathy and Freddie turned into more of a mixture of oil and water. Whatever the reason, Kathy's strong personality began to wear on Freddie. He began to increase his drug usage. The marijuana use turned into substantial cocaine use which eventually led to smoking crack.

Addiction can break up the best of relationships, and the more people are caught up in its web of disaster, the greater the chances of failure. Freddie and Kathy had constant fights and disagreements that at times became violent.

Anger often leads to a desire to get even. Such was the case on August 6, 1989, after an argument between Kathy and Freddie. She reported to Century Police Officer Gary Johnson that Freddie and a guy named Jim had just flown in a load of marijuana, and it was currently stashed at Timbo Campbell's residence.

What happened next is unclear. Her report was given to U.S. Customs Special Agent Dean Anderson to investigate. He soon learned his investigation was running right into the middle of an investigation run by his U.S. Customs colleague Ron Chambers and the DEA.

Anderson's investigation learned that a confidential informant (CI) in Belize had alerted U.S. Customs that Billy Dekle's Cessna 210 had been observed in San Pedro, Belize, on August 1, 1989, with its seats removed. The CI then relayed information to U.S. Customs that the same plane departed Belize on August 3, 1989.

Regardless of what occurred the night Kathy told Police Officer Johnson about the load of marijuana at Timbo's house, the loads continued to be brought in. As Freddie would learn, that was just the beginning of what anger would do.

Chapter 7

Violence

Patrolling the highways and dirt roads of northern Escambia County was what one made of it. At times, Deputy Ed Hudson would go from call to call without a break, but these reprieves were often few and far between.

Ed liked to stay busy, so when the calls weren't coming in, he liked to follow up on previous calls like burglaries and thefts. The midnight shift didn't really allow for these types of follow ups; however, it was a good time to round up people with warrants. Then there were some nights that were just good for patrolling.

On Sunday nights when the moon was bright, it became a planned event to leave Century and travel south on Highway 29 to Molino, a small community with a crossroad, a service station, a small grocery store as well as a store owned by the Wyse family, a post office, and two bars. The area's only claim to fame was that Don Sutton, a Major League Baseball player who had pitched for the Los Angeles Dodgers, had grown up there. In 1998, he was inducted into the Baseball Hall of Fame, and Molino paid tribute to Sutton by naming their Little League Baseball field after him.

Afterward, Ed would head north on Highway 97 to the Alabama state line at Atmore to check buildings along the way and to see if anything unusual was happening. Fortunately, it remained quiet and uneventful.

Then he would drive back west on Highway 4 to Century, checking those buildings along the way. This roundtrip excursion was completed without ever turning the headlights on. On nights with a bright moon, the eyes became adjusted, and it was easier to see further without the lights. Things that were moving could be spotted. Plus, others couldn't see him, which allowed the patrolman to possibly drive up on unsuspecting criminals.

This sixty-three-mile trip turned out to be relatively easy to complete without ever crossing the path of another vehicle.

During the midnight shift in the hot, early morning hours of August 6, 1989, Ed came across a pickup truck parked on the side of Highway 4 at the entrance to Lake Stone. Upon pulling over to check the vehicle, Ed discovered a young man's body lying on his side facing the road in the tall grass behind the pickup. He was of average size with brown hair and looked to be in his twenties. Foremost, Ed noticed he'd been beaten far beyond recognition.

As Ed tried to process this sight, he couldn't help to wonder if there was some natural reason he would be in this shape. He hated to think that someone could have done this much damage to another human being. But that line of thinking was fleeting as he realized this poor guy had probably been at the wrong place at the wrong time.

Ed placed his hands on the body, half-expecting to feel a cold corpse, but he was greatly relieved to find he was still alive. He immediately notified dispatch to send an ambulance.

While waiting, Ed searched the man for his wallet to find some kind of identification. His driver's license identified him as Donald

Woodford, which was confirmed by the pickup's registration. A few minutes later, the ambulance arrived.

Ed then began to survey the scene. It began to look like whatever happened to this young man had been done somewhere else. A beating this severe would surely have caused a disturbance in the tall grass, but none of it seemed pressed down except for where the truck had driven and parked and where the body had lain.

Within a week, rumors started flying in the small town of Century. The common thread in each one was Timbo Campbell and Bo-Bo Bell, a welder by day and partier by night during that time. They were supposedly the ones who had beaten Donald Woodford. However, rumors don't make for good evidence.

Woodford regained consciousness a few days later and had no recollection of what had occurred. Thus, he couldn't prove or disprove the rumors. The case was turned over to investigation, and Ed continued to patrol.

Thomas (Bo-Bo) Bell was Timbo's good and trusted friend. He knew all about Timbo's smuggling activities with Freddie. Even if he wasn't a part of it, he was often around it. On occasions, Timbo or Freddie would ask Bo-Bo to weld some hidden compartments in vehicles. He may not have been an "official" part of the organization, but Bo-Bo nevertheless liked excitement, and Freddie was willing to show him some.

On one of the trips in the later part of 1989, Bell went with Freddie to pick up a load in Belize, and excitement was served on the menu. Just to keep the entertainment going, Freddie decided to fly the plane upside down for what seemed like ten miles. Once Bo-Bo made it back home, he joined the ranks of those who said, "Never again will I get into a plane that Freddie Crow will be flying."

One morning in the fall of 1989, over nine years after becoming a cop for the Escambia County Sheriff's Department, Ed woke up with a sudden conviction that there had to be more to law enforcement. He had worked marijuana eradication cases with the Florida Department of Law Enforcement (FDLE), and he appreciated the way they worked.

FDLE had crews in various regions of the state that were assigned to marijuana eradication. It was their job to assist local agencies in locating and eradicating marijuana grown in their county. These crops were more commonly located in the rural areas, which included Escambia County where Ed worked. These were mostly seek-and-destroy missions, but occasionally, an arrest would be made. Some plots were carried out by hand while others required the use of the county dump truck.

He also had the opportunity to work with Terry (Hoss) Williams at the Alabama Attorney General's Office. Ed wanted to work bigger cases, but he first needed more experience to get there.

That evening in the den of their house, Ed talked with his wife Sharon about his desire to transfer from patrol to narcotics in the ECSD. In some ways, he felt like he had already asked enough from her to be married to a cop, but now he was asking her to be married to a narcotics investigator. This meant long hours, mostly at night, with cases that would call for road trips.

If this wasn't enough, Ed and Sharon were the parents of two daughters, one of whom was born with cerebral palsy. Her condition left her with the inability to walk or talk. The situation was difficult, and he wasn't sure if he should even ask.

It turned out to be an easy conversation. Sharon said, "When I married you, I knew I was marrying a cop. I see this as being part of it."

The couple said a few prayers. The next morning, Ed went into work and typed up a memo requesting a transfer to narcotics. Now it was just a matter of waiting to see what happened.

Lieutenant Roger Tyree delivered the word to Ed that he would be the next transfer into narcotics, but it would be January 1990, before the move could take place. Until then, routine patrol continued.

Although it seemed a little unusual to hear about the transfer two months in advance, Ed didn't ask any questions; he was just so excited with the news. What he didn't know then was that the narcotics unit was beginning a wiretap case and needed extra people to monitor the tapped telephone lines.

The loads continued to come in. Around the end of 1989, Dekle flew a Cessna 210 to pick up yet another load from Johnny Crawford, which ended up in a tragedy of great proportions. As routine, the plane landed on the remote strip in Belize. The engine continued to run while it was first refueled and then loaded with marijuana. One of the locals, who helped load the marijuana onto the plane, stumbled and fell into the turning propeller, causing the propeller to strike him in the head and splatter blood and brain matter onto the plane and those close by. As horrible as the situation was, there was really nothing else to do but finish loading the plane and try to make it back.

The blood-splattered plane limped onto Joe Jones's airstrip in Santa Rosa County with its bent propeller. The marijuana was offloaded, but the damage to the propeller was extensive, creating additional problems. The general consensus determined that it was too much for them to repair, so the plane would have to be dismantled and taken to professionals.

The steering cables were hacked with a hatchet, and the wings were removed and stored, along with bladder tanks, life rafts, and radio equipment, in a green block house owned by Joe Jones at the airstrip. They also stored the motor there as well as the fuselage, which was the main body of the aircraft that included the cargo area and pilot seating. Too many questions could come from looking at this damage. Dekle had contacts he trusted in South Florida, so it was transported there to be worked on.

Once the Cessna 210 was repaired, Freddie and Timbo transported the wings to South Florida, where they were put back on as best as they could be, and the plane was made ready for another trip.

Then on a cold Christmas Eve, 1989, Ed was on patrol. The north winds slammed against his vehicle, making him thankful he was inside of it. Its frame blocked the impact that would undoubtedly cut through any and all protective clothing.

Ed observed two pickup trucks parked on the back side of Pleasant Hill Baptist Church on Highway 29 just south of Century. Vehicles parked at a church on Christmas Eve would not be unusual, but it still was worthy of checking out, especially due to the cold weather. Inside those trucks could have been someone in need of assistance, members of the church, or the getaway vehicles for a burglary in progress. The situation stirred his curiosity, and now was time for a citizen contact.

As he drove up to the pickups, he noticed both vehicles were occupied, two males in one and two females in the other.

He approached the truck with the two males first since it was closest to him. He yelled for the inhabitants to roll down their window as he shined his flashlight into the glass pane. He tried to cover the surprise he felt when he recognized Timbo in the driver seat and Bo-Bo Bell in the passenger seat. He had come to know what they looked like from working in a small town.

With the Woodford case still under investigation and fresh on Ed's mind, alarm bells went off seeing the two together. There was still a possibility nothing was happening, but he certainly had reason to be cautious. Ed then shined his flashlight into the rest of the truck and observed the butt of a .22 caliber revolver sticking out of a holster that was attached to a western-style belt draped over the console.

Ed immediately stepped back and drew his service weapon. "Step out of the vehicle!" he ordered.

Both men complied without incident. Ed only had one set of handcuffs with him, so he improvised and used them to handcuffed both men. Handcuffing two people with one set of cuffs didn't give complete security, but it limited the subject's movement.

The best way to handcuff two suspects is to cuff the right hand of one subject to the right hand of the other, either by having one subject face you and the other looking away. Another way is to have both subjects face away from each other, pulling the right hand of the right subject behind his back and then pulling the right hand of the left subject behind the back of the right subject until both wrists were cuffed. It made running away extremely difficult.

A quick pat down for any other weapons was then made on both subjects as he positioned them away from the pickup. Finding none, Ed then looked in the pickup and quickly located two Glock 9mm handguns under the seat where Bo-Bo had been sitting. This turned out to be a mistake. The girls had exited their pickup and were standing with Timbo and Bo-Bo before Ed had realized it. He had no idea at this time the roles the girls had played. Ed found himself in a potentially dangerous situation, one he would not forget. Although the men were somewhat controlled, Ed had no idea what the girls had in the way of weapons on them.

After separating the four by placing Timbo and Bo-Bo in his cruiser, Ed then turned his attention to the two girls. They gave him permission to search their pickup truck, and nothing was found. Knowing Timbo was married, Ed found the girls guilty of nothing but poor judgement, so Ed allowed them to leave.

Both men were transported to the Escambia County Jail where they were booked for carrying a concealed firearm and open carry of a firearm, which was not allowed in the state of Florida

In January 1990, Dekle once again flew the Cessna 210 to Belize to pick up another load. However, the return trip was a disaster. When the previously dismantled plane reached Rancho Santa Teresita in Quintana Roo, Mexico, it could go no farther. It simply hadn't been able to recover, so it ended up crash-landing on the Mexican beach.

Dekle was able to walk away once again, which made it yet another good landing. When he made it back home, he told Freddie that as he walked away, he watched the Federales rush to the plane site, apparently more interested in doing some offloading and grabbing the marijuana for themselves than finding the pilot of the plane and arresting him. According to a U.S. Customs report out of Merida, Mexico, approximately 232 pounds of marijuana were recovered from the plane. Of course, we can only guess how much was actually recovered since only Billy Dekle and Johnny Crawford knew how much was on the plane, and they weren't talking about it.

Dekle made his own way back to Belize where he was able to contact Freddie to explain his predicament. Freddie had a trusted friend, Earl Garrett, fly commercial to assist Dekle by providing money for a ticket and food for his return.

Not having an airplane put a kink in running the next load, so that had to be addressed. To fix this dilemma, Dekle reached out to his old friends James McDonald, a pilot, and Travis Belshe, who had been assisting McDonald. Together, they located a Cessna 210 at the Enterprise, Alabama Airport that looked promising.

McDonald transported Dekle to the airport and dropped him off. Once entrance was gained by removing the hangar's metal siding, Dekle found a Cessna and used the one-size-fits-all Cessna key to crank it up and fly away.

He landed at Jones's airstrip where he stored the plane in the barn until it was made ready for flight. Joe Jones, Earl Garrett, and Billy Dekle installed the bladder tank.

On April 19, 1990, Dekle left once again to fly to Belize to pick up another load. The 600 pounds of marijuana were flown back to a secluded logging road in Liberty County where Jones and Garrett offloaded. The marijuana was transported to Century where it was stored at Joe Garrett's residence. The plane was abandoned on the logging road in the pine trees of Liberty County.

A few weeks later the FDLE Marijuana Eradication Team was looking for marijuana in Liberty County. Pilot Special Agent J.B. Dobson sat down to refuel. One of the ground crew, Special Agent Donnie Branch, asked him, "Have you seen anything yet?"

J.B. replied in his deep no-nonsense voice, "No, well, yeah, I guess I did. I found an airplane."

The plane was checked out, and J.B. flew it out of the woods. Special Agent Jessie Bruce Dobson became the first FDLE Special Agent to die in the line of duty. While searching for marijuana in Lake City, Florida, his rotors struck a guidewire to an antenna tower, causing his helicopter to crash. He was a tall man, known as the Gentle Giant, leaving behind a very large void.

During this time, Timbo's personal problems really began to take hold. He already had one case pending for the firearms charge that

Deputy Ed Hudson had previously arrested him for. Then the green-eyed monster—jealousy—took hold of him concerning his girlfriend Tina Storie.

Tina was at Justin's bar one night when Timbo arrived to see her sitting with two guys. Timbo called her outside, and that was when things turned ugly. He pointed a gun at Storie and declared that he was a jealous man and that he would kill her.

He then told Storie to get into his vehicle, and he took her home. Timbo's actions didn't go without repercussions.

Timbo and Bo-Bo ended up getting arrested on April 17, 1990, for the aggravated battery of Donald Woodford. When Ed asked Bo-Bo almost three decades later why they beat him, he said, "Because we were stupid."

Timbo's and Bo-Bo's trials were separate with Bo-Bo being the first one up. He was convicted for his role in the battery and sentenced to five years of house arrest followed by five years of probation.

Timbo was tried next. The defense strategy was that the guilty person was (Bo-Bo) Bell; he did the crime. It worked, and Timbo was found not guilty. Then on April 23, 1990, Timbo was charged with the assault on Tina Storie.

Timbo's legal woes caused him to be in jail during the April load, so he couldn't help, but Dekle paid him offloader's pay just the same like he had done for Glen Monroe. Maybe he felt sorry for him or was buying his loyalty. Dekle simply told Freddie he thought Timbo could use the money.

Dekle would try to help his people where he could. He would make sure they were taken care of if they were going through a rough time, even if they weren't able to help bring in the load. Sometimes he would try to help people just because he wanted to.

Such was the case when Billy Dekle showed up at Bobbie's residence one day. Bobbie met him at the door, and she could tell he had a box of teabags in his hand. Feeling very confident that he was not bringing her tea, Bobbie immediately told him to take the box and leave.

Dekle opened the box and revealed its contents—$40,000 in cash neatly stacked inside the box. He explained that the money was hers and that she could spend it any way she wanted. However, Bobbie was adamant—she didn't want anything to do with it and asked him to leave.

The organization was generous in other ways too. Freddie was known to empty the racks of T-shirts at Walmart when it came time for him to fly to Belize. The T-shirts were greatly appreciated by those who had so little. On one flight just before Christmas, Freddie bought a load of frozen turkeys, beef, and Bic lighters to give away to the natives. Freddie just liked to make people happy.

Unfortunately, Freddie was not keeping himself happy, though. The drug use had become so bad it had begun to ruin his life. The cocaine had created a paranoia to a point that he was not much use to the operation. Freddie eventually checked into the Twelve Oaks Rehabilitation Center at Fort Walton Beach. He wanted to take back his life.

Bobbie visited him at Twelve Oaks and tried to offer support. On one of the visits, Freddie requested that Bobbie bring Kathy Salter with her. Bobbie didn't see that as a good idea, but if Freddie wanted it, she would try to abide.

During the visit, Freddie and Kathy seemed to have a bit of a disagreement. On the way home, Kathy opened up to Bobbie in a way only she could. She explained that Freddie wasn't going to stay clean. She said she would have him back on the dope in a week once she got him home.

Bobbie wanted to stop and put her out of the car, but she just kept driving and took her back to Freddie's.

Kathy kept her promise. After Freddie was released, the drugs continued, and so did the fights.

Then on one hot June morning, a call came into the 911 operator—gunshot victim at 740 Freeman Road, Century.

Chapter 8

Rambo

On June 11, 1990, at 9:29 a.m., a call was received by the 911 dispatcher. There had been a shooting at the home of Freddie Crow.

Century Police Officer Greg Sutton responded along with Deputy Elvis "Tiny" Levoy. Because Freddie had already gained the reputation of a high-scale marijuana distributor, Narcotics Investigator Ed Hudson was also contacted at home and requested to respond with other members of the Escambia County Narcotics Squad. The initial concern was that the shooting could be drug-related. Drug wars could get out of hand quickly. It was also an opportunity for the narcotics squad to get a look into Freddie's personal life and possibly see evidence of his criminal activity.

When Ed arrived to the address given, he noted how nice the residence was by most standards. He walked over to "Tiny", who was talking to someone on a stretcher that had yet to be loaded into the open ambulance. Tiny was a large man by all measures, the size of a deputy anyone would love to have for backup. His salt-and-pepper hair made him appear to be in his early forties, and he wore glasses, which he continuously had to push back up onto his nose.

Ed walked over to Tiny as he discussed the incident with the stretcher's occupant, who happened to be Freddie Crow. Freddie and Tiny had attended Century High School together and were very familiar with one another.

Ed listened as Tiny conducted his interview, not wanting to interrupt. Freddie appeared to be angry, loudly proclaiming, "She shot me! Kathy shot me!"

Turning, Ed headed for the house to talk with the alleged shooter. Upon first sight, something was certainly amiss. Lamps were thrown across the room. A vase was lying broken on the floor. Everything was in turmoil.

He found a woman wearing a spaghetti-strap top and yellow shorts sitting at the bar just off from the den, fidgeting with her hands and acting very nervous.

Upon first glance, Ed was certain he had the right person, but just to be certain, he asked, "Are you Kathy?"

The woman looked up at Ed and then back down into her empty glass and resumed her fidgeting. "Yes."

He glanced around to assure no weapon was within reach of the woman. Satisfied, he said, "I'm Ed Hudson, an investigator with the Escambia County Sheriff's Department. Are there any more guns in the house?"

Kathy shook her head before raising it to answer. "Officer Sutton has the gun."

Ed glanced back to the front of the house before turning his full attention on Kathy. "What happened?"

"It was all an accident." Tears filled her eyes. "I would never do anything to hurt Freddie."

He glanced around at the nicely decorated home with what appeared to be the kind of decorating that had a place for everything despite the turmoil that presented itself.

Ed stayed with Kathy to wait for Crimes Against Persons Investigator Tom Martin to arrive. Kathy did her best to explain how it was all an accident, but as Ed looked around the inside of the residence again, he didn't see an accident.

Clearly, there had been a disturbance that ended in gunfire as confirmed by the bullet hole in the shattered window, the bullet hole in Freddie Crow, and by the only other person at the residence, Amos Jackson, a slender, African-American in his fifties who often worked for Freddie around the house.

Amos's demeanor was matter-of-fact when interviewed. He told Tiny, "I heard Freddie tell Kathy not to point the gun at him. Then Freddie turned to walk away. I saw Kathy doing something with the butt of the gun. Then it went off. I heard Freddie yell and saw him reach for the right side of his back. It was bloody."

Upon further investigation, it was determined that the bullet had travelled through Freddie's shoulder, hit a house plant, shattered a large glass window, and then hit a storage building outside.

The search for evidence continued at the residence. The scope was limited to what was in plain sight, and a lot of guns were in plain sight. Each one was cataloged and seized since Freddie was a convicted felon. According to Kathy, most of the guns belonged to Timbo.

Guns weren't the only discovery made that night. Ed was in the master bedroom when he noticed something just didn't look right about the bed. He peeked between the mattress and springs to see thousands of dollars stowed away.

Ed called for Sergeant Doyle Thomas to take a look at what he'd found. As Ed raised the mattress again, Sergeant Thomas said, "Damn." He stared at the money and shook his head. "Leave it alone; it's not in the scope of the search."

Kathy was taken to the Century Sheriff's substation where she gave a recorded statement to Investigators Martin and Ed. Kathy explained how she and Freddie had been having a disagreement over him staying out all night. She stated, "Freddie said he was leaving and was going to take the pistol with him. I saw the pistol on the VCR, so I rushed over there and grabbed it before he did. I didn't want him to take it with him. Then as Freddie walked away toward the door, I shoved the clip back into the butt of the gun, and it accidentally went off."

The next day, Freddie gave a statement saying it was all an accident, and he didn't want to press charges. In today's world, these circumstances would require the arrest of Kathy Salter, but this was 1990, and things were done differently back then.

Years later, Freddie would tell Ed how on that morning, he had announced that he was going to leave, to get away from her, and Kathy picked up the gun. He said, "I told her not to point that gun at me, but there was something in her eyes, in the way she looked at me, that I knew she was going to shoot me. I turned my back on her, hoping to put some distance between us, but it happened too quick. I felt the bullet rip through my shoulder. All I could think to do was run out the door before she could shoot again."

Someone, however, did go to jail. Investigator Martin applied for and received an arrest warrant for felony possession of a firearm for Freddie, not Kathy.

Freddie's arrest was made without incident. Resisting while still trying to heal from a hole in the shoulder was difficult. The incident caused great concerns for moving forward with his relationship with Kathy, as one would imagine. Freddie came to realize that she just wasn't the one.

About this time, another confidential informant met secretly with DEA Special Agent Charlie Gravat, U.S. Customs Special Agent Ron Chambers, and ECSO Narcotics Investigator Ed Hudson. Ed had been asked to come along due to having worked in the Century area and for his knowledge of the people involved.

The Informant began to tell about a group from Century that was involved with bringing in loads of marijuana by airplane. The CI told them that a guy named Jim worked with Freddie Crow, Timbo Campbell, and Earl Garrett. The agents, who had already been working the case for several years, were well aware that "Jim" was one of the aliases used by Billy Dekle.

The informant then conveyed how the four of them liked to hang out at Sammy's Gentlemen's Club on Gregory Street. But if we ever saw Timbo and Earl Garrett going to Pensacola together, we should check Bennigan's Restaurant behind University Mall. It was another favorite hangout for them as well as for the girls from Sammy's.

This was good information to tuck away as the case progressed, and that it did, and very soon afterward.

About two and a half months after Freddie's shooting, around two thirty on a warm sunny afternoon on September 27, 1990, Ed travelled south on Highway 29 headed to Pensacola to pay an informant for the previous night's deal. Because he was in a black Firebird with T-tops, Timbo and Garrett flew past him without realizing who (or what) he was.

Ed realized they could be going to Bennigan's. So after paying the informant, he drove over there too. Once in the parking lot, he began to look for familiar vehicles. He didn't see the vehicle Timbo and Garrett had been driving, but he did see a Mercury Grand Marquis with Tennessee license plate TDJ-618. This was a vehicle Gravat told him to look for. A quick registration check showed the vehicle to be registered to Jim Lang, Dekle's alias.

Ed's adrenaline spiked because he knew this could be a big break in the case. He also understood that he shouldn't confront these suspects alone.

He requested backup from his unit and then set up for surveillance. By the time backup arrived, Dekle had walked out to his vehicle and started to get inside it. Although he looked like most men as far as average height and build, it was his white hair that stood out amongst a crowd. Ed would know him anywhere. He pointed Dekle out by radio and told the units to close in.

Ed drew his weapon and approached from the front of the car as Dekle began to exit it. "Sheriff's Department. Freeze!" he ordered.

Dekle turned as if he was going to get back into the car. Ed didn't know what was in the car in the way of weapons. Plus, he didn't want Dekle to try to leave and then have to deal with a car chase.

Ed yelled, "Don't do it!"

Dekle paused before taking a step backward as if contemplating running. His eyes opened wide in complete surprise when he backed into the arms of Investigator Larry Scapecchi, who had come up behind him. Dekle was placed on the trunk of the vehicle and cuffed as he looked all around as if trying to find help.

As things began to calm down from the rush of adrenaline, one of the investigators, Scott Ricket, asked, "Now why are we doing this?"

Ed nodded his head toward the suspect. "That man is Billy Dekle. He's been a federal fugitive for about three years."

Scott tilted his head back with a nod and said, "Oh, I see."

Dekle hung his head with a very defeated look. There was nowhere to run, no way to escape, no need to resist.

A number of narcotics officers had responded when Ed called for backup. Now each one was scurrying around, assisting in securing the scene. Some prepared the vehicle for transport so it could be thoroughly searched at the narcotics office while another officer transported Dekle to jail.

Ed had additional duties, like notifying the federal agents of the arrest. His first call was to U.S. Customs Special Agent Dean Anderson. When he answered the phone, it sounded as though he had just woken up. Dean explained that he and his fellow Customs agents had been spending their nights doing surveillance on Joe Jones's airstrip in hopes that they would catch the plane coming in. When Ed told Dean he had Dekle, it was hard to tell what brought more relief, Dekle being caught or not having to sit up all night again.

Over the last three years, law enforcement had been building this drug smuggling case after learning the story behind the abandoned planes, bladder tanks, and the truck with a flat tire in Suwannee County, loaded with marijuana bales. It started with Glen Monroe's arrest and subsequent cooperation with law enforcement. Then Bruce Gibbs also started cooperating after his arrest.

The inevitable process of a case was unfolding. Enough information was obtained to present to a federal grand jury. Sealed indictments were then obtained for Billy Dekle and a person known only as Rambo.

Sealed indictments are usually obtained in ongoing investigations of the full scope of organizations that are still conducting criminal activity. The indictment assures an arrest, but the sealing of the indictment gives time for the investigation to determine the extent of the organization as far as who was in it and the role they played. Rambo was indicted because that is how he was known by those who cooperated. Now all that was left was finding out the full extent of the organization and who Rambo was.

Dekle was transported to the Escambia County Jail, and his vehicle was driven back to the narcotics office for inventory. Ed had already started on his way to the office when Sergeant Thomas called him on the radio. "You still at Bennigan's?"

"I just left, but I can go back. Why?"

Sergeant Thomas said, "The manager called into dispatch to report that when all the commotion was going on, a guy came into the kitchen trying to find the back door."

Ed spun his car around and drove back to Bennigan's. When he walked in the door, he found the manager standing with Freddie Crow.

Ed quickly assessed the situation. Why was Freddie still there? Why didn't he just run when he had the chance? "Are you lost, Freddie?" he asked.

Freddie fidgeted with his hands, appearing nervous. "I must be."

Ed and Freddie then walked outside and sat on a bench to talk. Ed asked, "Do you know Bill Dekle, the man we just arrested?"

Freddie shrugged, trying his best to act as if his being there was no big deal. However, his fidgeting increased, revealing that he was uncomfortable. "He's just someone I run into from time to time. What did you say his name was? I thought his name was Jim." His eyes kept darting toward his pickup, making it obvious he wanted to get in it and leave.

Ed then asked, "You okay with me searching your vehicle?"

Freddie nodded. "Yeah."

The vehicle was very clean, so Freddie was allowed to leave.

Although he was a known drug smuggler suspected of being *the* Rambo, law enforcement couldn't yet prove it. Freddie sauntered off without offering a goodbye, not even so much as a "Nice to have met you." Instead, he headed straight to his pickup and left.

Dekle's vehicle, on the other hand, proved to be a treasure chest of evidence. It had some cocaine in it along with a little marijuana, two pistols and ammo. But a very important discovery were the detailed ledgers, the two-way handheld radios, and thirty-eight dollars in quarters. The ledgers told the story of the loads of marijuana brought in. The radios were recognized as the kind used for ground crews to communicate with an airplane upon approach landing on a clandestine airstrip. The quarters were what every user of a payphone must have.

Illegal businesses must have communication. At a time when wiretaps were beginning to make their presence in law enforcement, it was best to use an unknown line for the telephone calls. For this organization, the answer was to use pay phones.

Following an arrest usually involved a mad rush of trial preparation. A speedy-trial rule requires cases to come to trial within ninety days. But in the United States District Court for the Northern District of Florida, the judges liked to speed things up a bit more. So the general rule was to be prepared for trial by thirty days. It kept the docket cleared and the attorneys on their toes.

This trial would be the first dance of several for this conspiracy. All of the physical evidence had to be brought in. Some of it was bulky, like the bladder tank and an actual marijuana bale from the Suwannee County load, which always made for good evidence. Some of it was not so bulky, like the photos of the abandoned airplanes, hotel records, and telephone booth records.

Still, it was the ledger taken from Dekle's car that was so damning. It not only revealed the amount of marijuana smuggled into our country, but who it went to and how much they got. It was often written in code, but there were ways to crack it, and that usually came in the form of cooperating defendants.

The subpoenas were sent out. The witnesses, which included law enforcement, civilians, crime lab personnel, and prisoners, began to come into Pensacola from all around, including Lake City and southern Alabama. They had agreed to testify as to their knowledge of the operation.

Donald Bossuyt, a farmer, Blayne Camp, an airplane mechanic, Jimmy Cash, the used-car dealer who sold Dekle his car, and suspects like Glen Monroe and Bruce Gibbs had made agreements with the government to provide truthful testimony concerning their participation in consideration for a lesser sentence. Each person was brought into the U.S. Attorney's Office where Gravat, Chambers, and Assistant U. S. Attorney Randall "Randy" Hensel interviewed them.

Hensel was an excellent attorney with an eye for detail, but what really seemed to make him great was the fact that juries just liked him. He was the son and grandson everyone wanted. He was also a collector and distributor of jokes. All of the agents knew he enjoyed a good joke, but if you ever told one to him, you had better be prepared to hear three from him.

During the interview with Glen Monroe the day before trial was to begin, he was able to provide an important missing piece to the puzzle—the identity of the camouflaged-painted, fatigue-wearing pilot. Law enforcement finally had what they wanted—enough evidence to arrest the notorious Rambo.

Chapter 9

Turn the Page

Exactly when Monroe learned Rambo's true identity was not exactly known. The agents didn't really care when he found out; they were just happy to have the answer. Now it was time to arrest Freddie Crow.

A mad scramble was occurring on the evening of November 6, 1990. Everyone knew they had only a narrow window when Freddie could be arrested. He had eluded law enforcement for so long with the name Rambo, and there was no telling what his plans would be about going on the run.

Initially, the investigation involved the DEA and Customs case agents because interstate and international drug conspiracies are best left to the federal agencies who have jurisdiction, which is determined by law. It includes not only the area of coverage, but the crime committed as well. This type of case called for the abilities and expertise of the DEA and Customs. It was the perfect case for the two agencies to work together since DEA is charged with investigating drug cases in general and Customs investigates drugs coming into the country.

As they began to make the arrest, they realized they needed assistance from the Escambia County Sheriff's Narcotics Unit to conduct a raid. Assisting other agencies was nothing new for this unit. They were staffed with expertise and a willingness to assist, which led them to be called upon often.

Law enforcement's forty-plus-mile trip to Century was made with a plan in hand. The raid would not be easy due to the fact the house sat on the back of the property that could only be reached down a long quarter-mile driveway.

Initially, the dark, starless night would be to law enforcement's advantage. Their vehicles came in as fast as possible. Freddie could hear the noise as the vehicles pulled behind the house. He could think of only one thing to do—run.

Out the back door, Freddie ran with DEA Special Agent Charlie Gravat close on his heels. Tales would later be told of Gravat's spectacular flying tackle that would rival the best of the NFL, but there was very little light to see. Gravat's account was that Freddie tripped, and he fell on him. However, the run was brought to an end. It was also the end of Freddie's freedom.

A search of the residence didn't reveal much of anything except for a box containing several books on how to disappear, change an identity, and literally become someone else. It confirmed the suspicion that Freddie was likely to go on the run. Someone with international connections and the ability to leave the country by simply flying away was of great concern. It would have been simply too easy for Freddie to elude capture.

Freddie was booked into the Escambia County Jail where he spent the night thinking. He knew he had done enough to warrant a life sentence. His poor decisions, lifestyle, and drugs had all but taken his life from him. Once again, he was faced with disappointing his family. It was time to make a change.

Bobbie had raised him in church, to have faith in God, but along the way, he decided to run from God and had been doing it ever since. He needed to come back to that faith, to come back to his senses.

The next morning, Freddie didn't ask to see an attorney; he asked to speak to the DEA. Overnight, he had made the decision to cooperate with the authorities and try to lessen his sentence, knowing all the while he was burning his bridges with the smuggling world.

Over the next few weeks, Freddie and Gravat became very familiar with each other. Numerous interviews lasting for hours were conducted.

Freddie tried to be as helpful as possible, considering he was working with a brain trying to recover from the effects of cocaine, but sometimes his efforts weren't enough for Gravat. At times when things started to heat up between the two, Freddie would look at the prosecutor and say, "Mr. Hensel, you better get him off my back, or I'll clam up!"

Hensel would say, "Charlie," and everything calmed down. Large segments of the interviews centered around the ledger found in Dekle's car. Freddie helped make sense of the code or abbreviations.

With Freddie's help, the agents were able to see how big the load was, who it went to, and who got paid for helping. One entry remained a mystery, so to speak. The initials "WLG" were next to some admittedly small purchases, but Freddie just couldn't remember who it was.

Those in the room—Gravat, Customs Special Agent Ron Chambers, and Florida Department of Law Enforcement Tim Robinson—were all just waiting for him to say William Lee Golden, but it never happened. Robinson saw a slight grin on Freddie's face when he reported his inability to remember. Hensel didn't see those small amounts purchased as being worth the time for prosecution, so all was well.

The interviews brought entertainment as well. Freddie talked about a problem they had with the bladder tank leaking in one of the planes and how they had to take it out and repair it.

FDLE Special Agent Robinson recognized the plane to be the one that was recovered on a dirt road in Liberty County. He also remembered that next to the pilot's chair was a battery with cables. So he asked, "Freddie, what was the battery for?"

"We hooked up the battery to the bladder tank when we needed to pump fuel out of it."

In a shocked voice, Robinson asked, "You mean you hooked cables to a battery in a plane with airplane fuel on the floor that leaked from a bladder tank? Weren't you concerned about the arc [an electric spark] blowing you up?"

Freddie shrugged. "We had a fix for that. We'd get the cable real close and then shove it onto the battery, so it was just a little arc."

That was just the way they did things.

The interviews were not the only thing going on. The conspiracy and distribution trial of Billy Dekle was in full swing. Witness after witness was called.

A subpoena had been sent to the Custodian of Records at the Enterprise, Alabama hotel. Some of Dekle's crew had stayed there during a trip to steal an airplane. A man dressed in khaki pants and uniform shirt showed up with the records. When asked who he was, he replied, "I'm the hotel janitor. I don't know why I'm here."

Apparently, the hotel sent the only "custodian" they had with the records. Thankfully, the defense didn't contest the authenticity of the records, and the janitor didn't need to testify.

The trial lasted for two days. The defense didn't present any witnesses, so the remainder of the trial was now in the hands of the jury. The evidence was overwhelming, so the verdict of guilty was not a big leap.

The holiday season was beginning. Almost everyone took days off from work except for the investigative team and of course, first responders. The fresh information obtained during Dekle's trial and the interviews with Freddie would need to be readied for a federal grand jury to obtain more indictments.

Now that Billy Dekle's trial was over, conspiracy charges were considered against a number of people, but only the ones with the best evidence against them would be selected. People like Randy Cannon, a distributor for Freddie in Alabama, was ever so close to escaping indictment. Unfortunately for Cannon, though, there was enough evidence to generate the interest of the DEA to the point that a search warrant was executed for his residence in Troy, Alabama.

The search revealed very little in the way of evidence, and the indictment didn't look promising. However, he just happened to be going through a divorce, and his wife made mention of a safety deposit box located in a bank in Troy. The court had already frozen the contents of that box due to the divorce proceedings. The soon-to-be former wife was not sure, but she believed it may contain money. Now a search warrant for that deposit box was prepared. When executed, its contents contained over $100,000.00 of unexplained cash. That finding caused the investigative team to look deep into his participation and ask additional questions. Sometimes, timing is everything.

On January 23, 1991, the federal grand jury for the Northern District of Florida delivered indictments for Johnny Crawford (the source of supply in Belize), Richard King (an offloader), Robert

Crawford (helped finance loads and provided a plane), Bruce Wilson, Jr. (offloader), Philip Cohron (offloader), Buddy "Indian" Davis (offloader), Hal Lee Walker (offloader with stash house), Bruce Gibbs's friends Bryant Cowart and Hal Walker (offloaders with stash house), James Adams (pilot), Clarence Earl Garrett (offloader), Joe Jones (owner of airstrip and barn used to store the plane), Otto Runkel (pilot), Timothy "Timbo" Campbell (offloader), and Randolph Cannon (distributor).

The four-count indictment included:

Count 1: Conspiracy to knowingly and intentionally import into the United States 1,000 kilograms or more of marijuana

Count 2: Conspiracy with intent to possess and distribute 1,000 kilograms or more of marijuana

Count 3: A substantive count of importation of over 1,000 kilograms of marijuana (a specific day and time the act occurred as opposed to the overall time frame)

Count 4: Possession with intent to distribute over 1,000 kilograms of marijuana.

Defendants didn't need to be in custody to be indicted by a grand jury. So, roundups of this size required planning and coordination, especially when going after a man with a reputation like Timothy (Timbo) Campbell. He required so much caution because he was considered a threat. So the multiple agencies consisting of the DEA, Customs, FDLE, ECSD, and ATF worked together for an arrest plan. Agents were paired together and placed in strategic points around Century. The plan was to locate Campbell and then report their findings to everyone else so a safe traffic stop could be made at a safe location.

In the early morning hours of February 11, 1991, Ed was roving since he knew the area and might be able to easily spot him. All was good until a voice came on the radio saying, "We've got him on Hecker Road."

Timbo's pickup truck was pulled over close to the entrance of the elementary school by two of the oldest deputies at the Escambia County Sheriff's Department—Lieutenant Louie Davis and Lieutenant Floyd Rose. They had partnered up and didn't need any help. By the time everyone reached them, Timbo was cuffed behind his back and bent over the hood of the vehicle.

While this was going on, multiple agencies also waited to snag Joe Jones and the others. Joe Jones was met by numerous police vehicles in Santa Rosa County as he traveled into Florida, from his cabin in Alabama. U.S. Customs Special Agent Dean Anderson pulled him from his pickup truck.

Joe Jones looked at Anderson and said, "I guess today is the day." He then told Anderson to look in the toolbox in his truck as he was placed in the back of a cruiser car.

Anderson asked FDLE Special Agent Supervisor Larry Smith to look in the toolbox in the driver side of the pickup truck while he checked the passenger side. Smith opened the lid to reveal a diamond-back rattlesnake coiled up and ready to strike.

Smith's fear of snakes was made known to all who were present. He yelled and began high-stepping it away from the truck as if he didn't know when to stop running. In reality, the snake had long lost its ability to strike, having had become the result of some very realistic taxidermy.

Of the fourteen people indicted, four became fugitives (Johnny Crawford, Robert Crawford, Richard King, and Bruce Wilson, Sr.), six pleaded guilty (Hal Lee Walker, Bryant Cowart, Clarence Earl Garrett, Otto Runkel, Timbo Campbell, and Randolph Cannon), and four went on to trial (Joe Jones, Philip Cohron, James Adams, and Buddy Davis).

Timbo agreed to cooperate with the investigation. He provided information that for the most part was consistent with what Freddie provided except for one thing—Timbo stated that Freddie's sister Bobbie was in charge of the finances for the organization.

This caused Bobbie to be brought in for an interview, which was very troubling for her. Billy Dekle insisted she had nothing to do with it and called out Timbo to be a liar.

Bobbie made no secret of her love for Freddie and how she would continue to stand by him during troubled times, but in no way would she aid him in any criminal endeavor. The agents found Bobbie to be very credible and completely discounted Timbo's account.

Timbo also gave a statement concerning the report made by Kathy Salter. He said that Century Police Officer Gary Johnson had called him to say, "… if you have at your house what I think you do, you better get rid of it." Johnson denied this claim to the investigating agents. Freddie confirmed to DEA and Customs that a load was flown in at the time Salter made her report, and it was stashed at Campbell's residence.

The trial of the four defendants, Joe Jones, Philip Cohron, James Adams, and Buddy "Indian" Davis was huge news for the tri-city area, so it caught the attention of the local newspaper, *The Tri-City Ledger*. The office was located in Flomaton and covered the news for Century and Jay as well. If it happened in the tri-city area, you could read about it in *The Tri-City Ledger*. The editor of the paper, Joe Thomas, covered every day of the eight-day trial. The May, 2, 1991, edition had such a complete, concise, coverage that prosecutors would later say that the article could have been used as a trial summary.

During this trial, Freddie testified to his involvement as well as to the involvement of all who participated. He explained how the organization paid $100 a pound for the marijuana and then sold it for $700 a pound with an overall average of 650 pounds a load.

When the organization was operating at full-capacity, they would usually run a load every other month. Once Freddie became a partner, he and Dekle would split the profits, which usually generated over $167,000 a load each. The offloaders were originally paid $10,000 a load but were later paid $15,000 a load. People like Joe Jones was paid $15,000 each time they used his airstrip, and then an additional $10,000 was paid if the plane was stored in his barn.

Blayne Camp testified he received $13,900 for repairing and working on airplanes for a man identified as Dekle. Camp testified that he did work for Dekle, but he didn't know him by that name. Instead, Dekle used the name "Doug Hanson." According to Camp's testimony, Hanson was a pilot who flew for a real estate company. Whereas Freddie had his camouflage, Dekle had his aliases.

Freddie would add that he and Dekle flew out of the FBO that Camp operated on several occasions for which Camp was paid an additional $10,000 to $15,000 each time. Freddie also admitted that he was a heavy cocaine user.

All four defendants—Jones, Cohron, Adams, and Davis—were found guilty. Each trial obtained additional information, and more people were indicted. As the case progressed, it came time to hand out the sentences. Judge Roger Vinson sentenced William Dekle to two life sentences. He said, "The only way you will ever leave the federal prison system is when your family comes to claim your remains." He eluded to the guidelines being high but that he had to adhere to them, and there was not a lot he could do about it.

Philip Cohron remained in the federal prison for eight years; Buddy Davis—eleven years; Hal Lee Walker—two years; Bryant Cowart—six years; James Adams—just under eight years; Clarence Garrett—eight years; Joe Jones—twelve years; Otto Runkel—eight years; Randolph Cannon—seven years; Timothy Campbell—just under five years. Johnny Crawford was indicted for his crimes but took advantage of the Belize policy of nonextradition of citizens and never faced justice.

On March 6, 1991, Freddie Wayne Crow appeared before Judge Roger Vinson for sentencing. DEA Special Agent Charlie Gravat appeared to testify that Freddie began cooperating within twelve hours of his arrest. Gravat went on to say that he spent several hundred hours interviewing Freddie and found him to be very truthful in providing information for other arrests and to other investigations.

Assistant United States Attorney Randall Hensel advised the court that Freddie's substantial assistance had to be in all caps for emphasis. He said, "This whole conspiracy ring we've been slowly unfolding with each additional defendant's cooperation … we're unfolding pages in the book one at a time, but when Mr. Crow decided to become a government witness and cooperate with us, we unfolded several chapters in one fell swoop."

Freddie also spoke to the judge, admitting his substance abuse problem, his decision to cooperate, and the difficulty in talking about people he had known his whole life. He also discussed the advantages in his decisions, of burning the bridge of going back to that lifestyle. In the end, he offered his apology to the courts and to the agents involved but also to his sister and family because of his involvement in smuggling.

Judge Vinson pointed out that Freddie was in a serious situation; he was looking at life in prison. However, the judge recognized the considerable assistance provided to the investigation and the fact that Mr. Hensel had gone as far as he had ever seen him go in speaking on someone's behalf. He also noted that he didn't seem to think it was so much about the money as it was the thrill of doing it and getting away with it.

He realized Freddie had already received a break of sorts due to the fact that the quantity of marijuana was underestimated as to what it really was. There were estimates that the organization was responsible for more than forty loads. Finally, Judge Vinson agreed that Freddie Crow had substantially assisted the government and sentenced him to ten years.

Robert Crawford and others were indicted and remained fugitives for some time. This is how Special Agent Tim Robinson of the Florida Department of Law Enforcement (FDLE) came into the case. Robinson made it his goal to first find Crawford with the help of some Texas Rangers who knew of a confidential informant (CI) with some knowledge of Crawford.

Once Robinson made contact with the CI, an opportunity presented itself to make a big round up by doing a reverse sting. A reverse sting occurs when a person, or persons, are actively seeking to perform an illegal act. Law enforcement, acting in an undercover capacity, provides services to carry out that act. In this case, Crawford and his associates were actively seeking to buy a load of marijuana. The CI made it known that a source was available with a load, and the sting was on.

Agents were brought into Tallahassee from Pensacola to Jacksonville. Crawford picked the location for the buy, and law enforcement just happened to be good with it. The load of marijuana was located in an old tobacco barn on County Road 12 north of Tallahassee.

Just as the operation got started, rain fell in sheets, creating floods that could rival those in the days of Noah's Ark. At that point, there was a mad dash just to get everyone rounded up.

The sting operation resulted in ten defendants sitting in one trial. The courtroom became crowded. At least half of it was filled with defense attorneys and their clients. Some of the defendants, like Robert Crawford, had a lot to lose. Then there were those defendants, like Lee Eastman, an offloader for one load, who were considered small fish in the pond of defendants.

As one would imagine, the trial took several days. The government presented its case, and then the defense—all of them—presented theirs. Once the defense rested, the judge allowed a short recess, and then court reconvened.

Before the jury was brought back in, Judge Vinson did a quick perusal of the courtroom and noticed that Lee Eastman was not present. The judge then asked Eastman's attorney, Joel Fanning, where his client was. Fanning replied something to the effect that he could only assume that Eastman saw the handwriting on the wall.

The judge decided to carry on with Eastman's absence. He made the comment that there were enough people sitting at the table that he didn't think the jury would miss him. The judge was very careful to warn Mr. Hensel not to make a comment about his absence since it could have prejudiced the jury.

All ten defendants were found guilty. Lee Eastman has not been seen by the authorities since.

Freddie went to prison, and in 1993, Ed Hudson became a Special Agent with the Florida Department of Law Enforcement. Ed inherited his first case from his supervisor Larry Smith (the one who was afraid of snakes). It involved a marijuana and cocaine dealer in Jay, Florida, by the name of Buddy Brunson. Buddy grew his own variety of marijuana called the "Coldwater Crippler." Those who "tried it out" said it was some of the best.

Richard Holloway, a person who sold marijuana for Buddy, testified against Buddy. Holloway seemed happy-go-lucky enough. Mr. Hensel asked him on the stand if he ever had any complaints concerning the marijuana.

Richard replied, "Oh yes, sir."

Surprised somewhat to hear this, Mr. Hensel asked, "How so?"

Richard said, "They brought it back 'cause it scared them. It made them see things."

The jury could not refrain from laughing.

Freddie had done business with Buddy Brunson, mostly for cocaine, so he was brought back to Pensacola again to assist in the investigation. During this time, Ed spent more time with Freddie in interviews.

As they sat across from each other at the conference table, Ed noted an improvement in Freddie's appearance and an ability to recall. Beforehand, he seemed to be in a bit of a fog. Freddie attributed the improvement in his health to being away from cocaine use.

The interview began with Freddie saying he held no ill will against the agents and investigators who worked on his case. He went on to say that in many ways, they may have saved his life by taking him away from his life of drug abuse.

Ed began to realize that the real stories told by Freddie were actually better than the ones he had heard but hadn't necessarily happened, at least not in the way they had been told. He just had to find out all about those stories in this first interview as an agent. Whereas before when he was with the ESCD, he mostly observed other agents interview Freddie.

Ed was able to pick up on certain motions Freddie went through when beginning to answer the first questions asked in the interview. A poker player would call it a "tell," a change in behavior or demeanor giving clues as to what was about to happen. The motions were like the prelude to a confession.

When the agents asked a question, he noticed how Freddie would sit up straight in his chair, look down at the table, raise his eyebrows, and then place his right hand flat on the table in front of him. He would then move it in a counterclockwise motion and usually wouldn't stop until the first question was answered. His actions resembled those of a little boy kicking the dirt as he confessed his misdeeds.

Now Ed was the interviewer. Up until this point, he hadn't really had an opportunity to get to know Freddie. Their meeting at Bennigan's was not an appropriate setting. Furthermore, Freddie's flying antics were the last thing on his mind at that time. So, the first question he asked was, "I heard you flew under the Highway 4 bridge going to Jay. Is that true?"

In a very matter-of-fact way, Freddie said, "No. I measured it, and there just wasn't enough room, but I'll tell you what I did do." Then he began to talk about some of the stunts he'd pulled in a plane, like flying under the pipeline on the Escambia River while painters hung on as best they could. He would take friends for rides that would totally end their flying experience for life.

At the end of the trial, when Buddy Brunson and his cocaine supplier Leon Dassinger, a.k.a. Joe Foster, were convicted, Ed transported Freddie back to prison in Eglin. As Ed drove, he began to talk to Freddie about various things, but mostly about setting his life right, putting the trouble behind him.

Ed said, "Freddie, why don't you write a book about your life?" It wasn't like he had a lot of other things to do.

Freddie shrugged. "Yeah, I've thought about it. Bobbie asked me to do the same thing."

By the time they reached the gates of Eglin, Freddie turned to Ed and said, "I'd like to stay in touch. Would it be all right if I called you?"

Ed nodded. "That's fine." He didn't know if Freddie would actually call him, but it certainly wouldn't hurt if he did. It could possibly lead to information coming out of the prison as the result of other inmates talking.

Looking back, Ed figured Freddie had made a conscious decision at this time to change who he associated with. Plus, Ed made a point to show an interest in Freddie by talking to him about turning his life around.

As Freddie got out of the vehicle, he said, "Good. Then I'm going to do that."

In 1995, tragedy hit Freddie's family. Thirty-two years earlier, Bobbie and her husband Lou had adopted a baby boy, Lou, Jr. Freddie had always been fond of Lou, Jr., and felt drawn to him because of the obstacles he faced in life as a result of being gay. He saw the struggles that Lou, Jr., encountered, and he always tried to let him know he was loved for who he was. Lou's sexual orientation wasn't hidden. Sometimes it was dealt with in humor.

Freddie once told Lou, Jr., that he was afraid to try being gay because he might like it, and then he would be in the same mess. Then Freddie gave a big smile, which resulted in laughter from Lou, Jr.

Freddie offered more than humor for help, though. Lou, Jr., expressed an interest in writing, so Freddie took it upon himself to purchase him a computer. In the 1980's, that was not a small gesture.

Lou, Jr., eventually fell victim to HIV which later turned to AIDS. His death was a loss felt by many and a loss for Freddie to endure alone in prison.

The calls came to Ed from Freddie, not very often, but it was like an old friend who called from time to time. Freddie would say, "I just called to check in."

Each call gave Ed a little more hope that Freddie's decision to change was sticking. It also gave Ed a chance to obtain a little more information from him, if not about a particular case, then about the drug business in general. They were good conversations.

As time went on, the conversations turned to getting out of prison. Then one day, Freddie said, "Listen, I just want you to know I'm through with all that, and if you ever need anything, you just let me know."

Ed couldn't help but feel good about that. A law enforcement officer likes to think he's made a difference. He likes to have successes, and Ed really wanted Freddie to be a success.

The last call from prison came with a request. Freddie wanted to know if it would be all right if he came to see Ed when he got out, and that was how this unexpected friendship started and the relationship grew.

Chapter 10

Sandra

On March 22, 1999, Freddie Crow became a free man. Although he was well-known for what he had done, his friends for many years, Jimmy and Rita Crowley, opened their home to him to stay with them. They had known Freddie Crow through all of his troubles and would even go see him while he was in prison.

Probation required Freddie to have a job, so he would begin working in a kitchen washing dishes. When he wasn't at work, he reconnected with childhood friends like Wayne Simpson.

Wayne came home from serving our country in the United States Army while Freddie was still in prison. As serving in the military will do, he came back with confidence and carried himself well. After adjusting to being home, Wayne began studying to be a barber at Carnley's Barber Shop in Flomaton, Alabama.

While Wayne was working at the barber shop, Freddie walked in. Without saying a word, he walked up to Wayne and wrapped his arms around his small frame. Wayne may have been tough and rugged, but he was nevertheless the kind of man to melt from the hug of an old friend.

Freddie then looked Wayne in the eye and said, "I'm sure glad I found you."

Wayne wasn't the only one Freddie sought out. He wanted everyone to know he was through with his old life. For this purpose, he went to see Judge Billy Ward, a retired county judge everyone had a great deal of respect for. Freddie stopped in to see Randy Hensel at the U.S. Attorney's Office. He kept his promise to Ed Hudson and went to see him at the FDLE Office. He made many visits to many friends like Tony Fore and Ricky Carnley from his childhood and Butch Watson and Mike Godwin, all of whom represented Freddie's efforts to surround himself with good people.

Freddie even called up Joe Thomas of *The Tri-City Ledger* and asked to come see him. Joe had some concerns at first, but he met with him anyway. Freddie just wanted him to know that his life of smuggling was over and to assure him there were no hard feelings about the newspaper article. They discussed the case and what had happened. The conversation lasted two hours. When it was over, Joe felt it was two hours well-spent.

It was a good time to reconnect with good people, and his time with family seemed to mean the most. There was his sister Bobbie, who never gave up on him, and Bobbie's husband, who he had nicknamed "Lou Baby," as well as his older brother Hurston and his wife Mary Ann.

However, fences would have to be mended, and Freddie knew it. Bobbie's daughter Darlene, for one, could not have been more done with him since his last arrest. It was hard for her to forgive, knowing what Freddie had put her mother through. Then there was the issue with his younger sister Tricia and her Alabama State Trooper husband

Harry. It was time to let bygones be bygones. He loved Tricia and wanted to be close to her again. Freddie had his work cut out for him, and he knew it.

He also was a very forgiving person, and this extended to his mother as well as his stepfather. It had to help to know that before Fred had passed away, his dad had found a way to get along with them too.

Friends and family were not the only people to whom he openly talked to about his mistakes. Freddie told most people he came into contact with who he was and what he had done. He didn't do it to brag but just to let them know, giving them the opportunity to end the conversation if they chose.

Freddie attended a fly-in at the Brewton Airport. A fly-in is an event where pilots can bring their planes and set them up for display. People often bring their specialty cars as well. As Freddie walked around the grounds taking in all the sights, he came upon two gentlemen gazing at a plane.

Never one to meet a stranger, Freddie began talking to them about the plane and how if he ever got his license back, he would love to have one like it. One of the gentlemen inquired as to what happened to his license. The man was a retired military pilot and a current commercial airline pilot.

Freddie said, "I had a problem with the FAA," and then went on to tell them about his drug smuggling activities and how he had flown loads into the surrounding area. He even described how he had flown to Texas, and brought back golf bags full of marijuana, landing at the Pensacola Airport. Freddie would exit his plane with his golf bag, having never played a game of golf in his life.

Little did Freddie know, the other gentleman was already aware of his whole story. He was DEA Special Agent Claude Cosey, the same

Claude Cosey who was a deputy sheriff in Escambia County, Alabama, when he found the bale of marijuana lodged high up in the pine tree. The two men listened to Freddie as he described his adventures in detail. They even talked about Freddie one day writing a book.

One thing that did not go his way was his attempt to regain his pilot's license. Freddie had petitioned the Federal Aviation Administration to have it restored. What he loved to do most was fly, but getting his license back just didn't happen. The rules were very clear—anyone who smuggled with an airplane did not get to keep their license.

Another disappointment came when Freddie attempted to locate some of his buried PVC pipe. Once upon a time, money was plentiful and had to be kept tucked away in a safe place for future use. Freddie had decided to put money in sealed PVC pipes and bury it in various locations in the woods. The plan was to identify landmarks, like trees and stumps, so it would be easy to find them when he returned.

What Freddie didn't count on was 1995. He was still in prison when Hurricane Erin, a Category 2 hurricane, hit the Gulf Coast in August of that year. Then Hurricane Opal, a Category 4 hurricane, hit in October. By the time 1995 was over, nothing looked the same. Trees had fallen. Land had been cleared. The landmarks were gone, and so was his ability to locate the money.

However, what proved to be anything but a disappointment was Sandra, the friend and coworker Rita kept talking about and wanted Freddie to meet. Sandra Cartwright was born the youngest child and only girl to William and Esta Mae Cartwright. She grew up in Pensacola, Florida, with her parents and two brothers and attended J.M. Tate School. During high school, she served as chaplain of the Pep Club and was a member of the Future Homemakers of America.

Sandra was a quiet, soft-spoken Southern belle with a radiant smile and deep-set hazel eyes. Although slow to anger, she could be worked up to a good foot stomp. Sandra was not without ambition. Her goals in life were to have one of three careers: photographer, flight attendant, or nurse. One of these would later become a driving force within her that gave her purpose.

William and Esta Mae made sure their children attended church, so the family could often be found at the Cottage Hill Assembly of God on Sundays. This upbringing brought a fear of God into her and respect for her parents, which carried on into adulthood.

At the age of eighteen, Sandra met and fell in love with Charles (Charlie) Scott. Charlie was six years older than her. As days went by, and date followed date, the more time they spent together, the closer they were drawn to each other.

On July 21, 1974, at the age of nineteen, Sandra and Charlie were married and lived in Pensacola. Charlie, a slender man with wavy, brown hair, worked in grocery stores where he climbed the promotional ladder to the position of manager. The first six years of the marriage were good years by any standard. Charlie didn't want Sandra working outside of the home, so she became a homemaker.

They seemed to adjust to the changes that came with married life, and their time together was cherished. Their union brought forth two children—Melissa, who was born in May 1976, and Michael, who arrived in January 1980. Then after the birth of Michael, things seemed to go downhill in the marriage.

The unfortunate and not so unique growing apart began to happen. Charlie spent much of his time at work, and Sandra's whole life revolved around the home and the children. As time passed, the distance became farther and father. The next eighteen years proved to be very difficult.

Charlie and Sandra moved to the Century area in the early 1980s. Sandra became very close friends with one of Charlie's nieces, Sherry Scott. Sandra went to Sherry in order to escape the despair that comes with an unhappy marriage.

At this time, Sandra worked as a nurse's aide for Dr. John Vanlandingham in Flomaton, Alabama. This job gave Sandra another very close friend, Rita Crowley. Sherry and Rita gave Sandra the support she needed during this difficult time. When Sandra left Charlie in 1997, and finally obtained the courage to file for divorce, the situation continued to go downhill. Charlie didn't take the breakup very well. A restraining order was issued, and the papers were served by Deputy Randy Murph.

When Randy advised Charlie he had a restraining order to give him, Charlie stared blankly. Randy then read the order to him and explained what it meant to the best of his ability.

The instructions were not quite clear enough for Charlie. He ended up sending flowers to Sandra. As well-intentioned as those flowers may have been, it still represented contact, and contact was considered a violation of the restraining order. Consequently, he was ordered to attend anger management courses in Pensacola. The divorce became final in 1999.

Around the year 2000, Rita felt that what Sandra needed was a man in her life and felt like she knew just who that should be. Freddie still lived with Rita and Jimmy Earl. She talked about Freddie to Sandra in hopes they would meet. However, Sandra had heard about Freddie Crow, and she was pretty sure he was the last person she needed to get tied up with.

After a great deal of persistence, Rita finally managed to get Sandra to stop by for dinner one evening. Freddie was cooking spaghetti, and Rita had raved about it so much that Sandra decided to give it a try.

Also present for dinner was Jimmy Cash, the car dealer and one of the local Century boys who really fancied himself as a lady's man. The dinner went well, and Freddie really seemed to like Sandra, even though he would later tell her that his "rival" Jimmy Cash was absolutely certain that Sandra had spent all of her time looking at him instead of Freddie.

Admittedly, Sandra was very impressed with Freddie, but still, she couldn't get past his bad reputation. As for Jimmy Cash, well, she had no desire for him.

Rita continued to try to play matchmaker, but Sandra resisted. After all, this was Freddie Crow they were talking about, and good girls did not go out with Freddie Crow, at least not in public. This didn't deter Freddie from asking Sandra out. It eventually came to a plea for help that would bring them together.

Around 11:30 on a relatively warm night in late March 2000, Sandra was by herself driving to meet a friend. She pulled down to a gravel lake off Old Flomaton Road, and her car got stuck in the sand. As she got out and evaluated the situation, she realized she wouldn't be able to get her car out of the sand without help.

However, she knew that being in this location at this time of night all alone looked so peculiar that she couldn't call just *anyone*. It had to be someone who wouldn't judge her or someone whose opinion of her didn't really matter. It had to be someone who had done much worse than whatever you could do to get stuck at the gravel lake at midnight. Since her friend couldn't meet her at the last moment, the only person she could think to help her was Freddie Crow.

Sandra placed a call to Rita's home. After Sandra asked to speak to Freddie, Rita squealed with excitement and then giggled. The sound of her feet could be heard scampering throughout the house as she ran to Freddie's bedroom.

Freddie took the phone, and Sandra explained to him where she was and what had happened. He acted like he didn't understand. "Now, where are you?" he asked. "I'm not sure I know where that is."

The whole idea of Freddie not knowing where Sandra was describing was preposterous; it was in an area he had spent his whole life. After talking a little bit more, Freddie told her to call back in five minutes.

She did. Freddie said, "I was hoping you wouldn't call back. Tell me again what had happened."

Sandra was at his mercy and attempts to play hard to get. She repeated the information to him and then asked, "Are you going to help me or not?"

Freddie continued to act like he still wasn't sure where she was. Sandra then gave him step-by-step instructions on how to get where she was, starting from pulling out of Rita's yard.

Freddie asked, "Did you get stuck just turning around? I might have been born at night, but it wasn't last night." He couldn't help but smile to himself. "Okay, I'll come help you out."

Upon arriving, Freddie assessed the situation and decided they had to go borrow a truck from his stepdad Buddy. She rode with Freddie to get the truck. When he got out, Sandra overheard him tell Buddy that his girlfriend had gotten stuck, and he had to pull her out. For Sandra, that sort of added insult to injury.

They returned to the scene of the stuck car. Before they could free the vehicle, Freddie and Sandra had to get down on their knees and dig the sand away from the tires by hand. Eventually the car was freed. They both were sweaty and sandy. Sandra felt relieved and grateful.

"Thank you, Freddie Crow," she said and kissed him on the cheek.

Using a serious tone, Freddie said, "Just call me *Wrecker Man*. What I ought to do is throw you in the back of that car and collect my payment."

Sandra believed him. Now scared, she wondered if she should scream, but who would hear her? Should she run? She knew she couldn't get away.

Then Freddie broke into a huge grin. "Get in that car," he said, "and don't stop until you get home."

Feeling relieved yet again, Sandra jumped into her car and took off.

The inauspicious stuck car incident led to Freddie calling her the next day to ask her out on a date. After the first date, Sandra knew she saw something in him, something a lot of people didn't see. He was actually a good man who treated her with respect. He was definitely worth pursuing; however, there was one big problem. How could she break the news to her mother Esta Mae that she was dating Freddie Crow? The news would certainly lead to disaster, and there was no way to change that. The best she could do was to pick the right place and time to tell her.

It turned out that Sandra knew her mother very well. She met her mother at a place where they could be alone. Hopefully, her mother would be in a good mood. Upon breaking the news, however, her mother's reaction was just short of a heart attack. Fortunately, every-one—including Esta Mae—who learned of this relationship did survive the initial reaction.

In the meantime, Freddie maintained his job washing dishes at Morrison's Restaurant in the Town and Country Plaza in Pensacola. At his first opportunity, he began truck driving school. Sandra, wanting to improve her position, enrolled in Reid State Nursing School. Between school and work, the couple didn't have a lot of time to get to know one another, but they did the best they could.

Freddie obtained his commercial driving license and then used the trucking business to reconnect with people who lived out of town. When close to the Phoenix City area in Alabama, Freddie began stopping by Tricia and Harry's. Soon, the work to mend fences began to pay off. His visits turned into overnight stays, and the family began to bond again.

The trucking job helped to mend another fence. Freddie knew he was going to be in Mobile, so he decided to give his old friend Rocky LeBlanc a call. By now, Rocky was on the city council for Mobile and doing quite well for himself.

When Rocky first got the call, his suspicions ran wild. After all that had happened and after all this time, why was Freddie Crow wanting to talk to him now?

Nevertheless, he agreed to meet. Freddie grinned ear to ear when he saw the clean-shaven, tall friend with thinning black hair and heard his southern voice. Rocky saw an old friend who was sincere when he said he had put his past life behind him. It wasn't difficult for two people who truly cared for one another to come back together.

All of those events of the past seemed to have never happened. Rocky invited Freddie into City Hall, where afterwards everyone often asked when Mr. Crow was coming back? Freddie and Rocky became inseparable. They had many more meetings and many, many more telephone calls.

Sandra wanted to celebrate getting her own checking account, so she and some friends went to Jalisco's, a Mexican restaurant in Brewton, Alabama. She ordered a margarita.

The waiter, speaking in broken English, wanted to know if "Senorita want another? Senorita got to drive home? I drive you home," he offered with a big smile as he mimicked driving with his hands.

Sandra told Freddie all about it the next time she saw him. Freddie, a bit concerned, said, "Hmm. Who is this guy? Tell me what he looked like?"

By this time, Freddie had started driving cross-country for his new job. Sandra returned home one night to see a message on her answering machine. As she listened to it, she heard a man speaking with a Mexican accent. He wanted to speak with Senorita Sandra Scott.

Sandra didn't know what to think. She was certain this message had to be from the waiter at the Mexican restaurant. He apparently got her number from her check. What was worse, he now had her address as well.

The anxiety only increased when this message was followed up by two more. Sandra really did not know what to do.

A few days passed, and Freddie returned home. He was driving her down the road one evening when he informed Sandra she had failed the test.

She had no idea where he was going with that statement. Worried that Freddie thought she had done something wrong, she asked, "What are you talking about?"

Freddie asked, "Why didn't you tell me about the waiter from Jalisco's calling you?"

Sandra was dumbfounded. How did he know?

Freddie said, "I'm the one who called you and left those messages." He then rolled a few words in Spanish off his tongue, ending with a big grin.

Sandra spent the next few minutes very relieved while simultaneously trying to decide if she should be angry at Freddie or not and exactly what she should do with this guy.

DEALING WITH ESTA MAE

On July 13, 2001, another sad event occurred for the Crow family. Freddie's mother Sybil passed away from heart failure. Freddie loved all of his family, but a mother is always special. He knew the trials he had put her through, the worry he must have caused her when raising him—the time he shot himself in the foot, running multiple loads of marijuana, the acrobatics his plane performed while he piloted it, and the number of arrests and all of her trips to the prison to visit him. For all of that, he was sorry. He had come to speak of her fondly, especially when he talked about how much she loved to fish.

Sandra's mother was more complicated. As Sandra and Freddie grew closer and closer, they would have to jump over another hurdle with Sandra's mother.

Freddie and Sandra had decided to live together. Sandra knew her mother wasn't going to be happy with her moving in with any man she wasn't married to. The news was going to go over about as easy as telling her she was going out with Freddie.

Her mother's immediate response was scorn. Sandra quickly tried to defend her actions by pointing out that she had already been burned once. Esta Mae was just as quick to point out that if she did this, she would burn again. Nothing like having fire and brimstone heaped upon you.

Freddie did his part to smooth things over in ways only Freddie Crow could do. He made frequent calls to Esta Mae. Sometimes, he called to simply check on her. Then other times, he pretended to be the police calling because they had received a complaint of loud rock music coming from her house, disturbing her neighbors.

Then about a year after they moved in together, Freddie proposed to Sandra. It really didn't come as a big surprise, just kind of a natural progression. However, it prompted a different call to Esta Mae.

Freddie enjoyed calling people and pretending to be someone else. Whereas before, he had called Esta Mae pretending to be the police.

This time, he pretended to be Reverend Johnson as a hoax to stir up Esta Mae.

They started the conversation exchanging pleasantries. Then the "reverend" told her that Freddie and Sandra had asked him to perform their wedding ceremony. He began going over the plans. "I understand the wedding is to take place at the Homestead Lounge in Molino," he stated matter-of-factly in his soft, reverend voice. The Homestead Lounge was a country bar, out in the country, frequented by, well, country people, and only the exact opposite of what Esta Mae had in mind for her only daughter's wedding.

Esta Mae's eyes popped wide open in surprise. Loudly, clearly, she yelled, "*What? No!* Who told you that?"

Freddie started laughing, and Esta Mae recognized the voice. It didn't belong to the reverend but to Freddie. It was the kind of thing she learned to expect from him.

In the end, this kind of teasing and personal attention won over Esta Mae because she did have a sense of humor. Freddie had become one of Esta Mae's favorite people.

So, on September 21, 2002, Sandra became the first and only Mrs. Freddie Crow.

Chapter 11

The Next Sentence

The wedding occurred at the Flomaton Community Center, not the Homestead Lounge. It was a beautiful event complete with a reception.

The crowd was all gathered inside and waited on the newlyweds' entrance. As Freddie and Sandra arrived and greeted the guests, Freddie dragged one leg as he pulled a plastic ball and chain that was attached to his ankle. Then he approached the front and announced, "This is about to get real!"

Sandra responded to Freddie's antics by bringing out a rope with a noose tied to the end. She promptly wrapped it around Freddie's neck.

The guests loved it. At the end of the reception, Bobbie insisted they all go to Jalisco's in Brewton. She wanted to make sure they knew Sandra was a married woman. The Jalisco's incident would go on to be a family joke for some time to come.

By 2003, Tricia's daughter Heather added to the family by marrying Josh Hudson. Josh became a special person in Freddie's life. Freddie pretty much liked everyone unless he detected a mean spirit. Then he just wouldn't have anything to do with them. But if he gave them a nickname, that meant they were special.

Freddie gave Josh the nickname of "City Boy." He reminded Freddie that he really didn't live in the city, but it mattered not to Freddie. He always referred to him as City Boy, and Heather and Josh became one of Freddie's favorite couples.

Tricia's son Bryan was in, visiting with family, and then he would be out doing his own thing. He later became involved with rodeos and horses, which kept his time more occupied. Freddie didn't get to spend a lot of time with him.

Freddie also had other nieces and a nephew, but he didn't spend much time with them either. His brother Hurston and wife MaryAnn had three children. Their son Allen followed his dad's lead and worked in the National Park Services. Their daughters RuthAnn and Alison lived too far to visit.

Freddie's relationship with Bobbie never faltered. She was the binding that held the family together. Although Bobbie's daughter Darlene had been very angry with Freddie after his last arrest, the love between the two won over.

Life for the Crows was off to a good start. After four long years of driving a truck, Freddie started his own concrete finishing business. L.J. Carnley, a man Freddie had respected since his youth, had decided to sell his business—West Florida Concrete Coat. They could make the finish on a concrete slab look anyway you wanted it to look, giving it finishes such as brick, tile, or wood.

L.J. showed Freddie the ins and outs of the business, and Freddie was making beautiful finishes in no time. This opportunity allowed Freddie to get off the road and stay at home with Sandra, where he wanted to be. It was a good business, and business was good. In fact, it was thriving.

Sandra had finished first in her nursing class at Reid State. In 2004, it was time to look for a house, a place they could call their own.

The house Freddie and Sandra fell in love with, the perfect place, was right next door to the perfect neighbors, Wayne Simpson and his wife Diane. Freddie and Wayne Simpson had come full circle in their friendship. They started out life together as neighbors when they were kids, remained friends, and now they were neighbors once again.

Wayne jokingly told Freddie that he was going to put up a concertina wire fence (also known as barbed wire or razor wire) so that Freddie would feel at home. Freddie could only laugh.

The Crow's mortgage application was made, and the loan started processing. Then on September 2, 2004, Hurricane Ivan wreaked havoc on the Gulf Coast around Pensacola. The storm caused serious roof damage to the house that would need to be repaired before the sale could go through. As a result, the sale was delayed until the end of the year.

Buying the house had been a big step in both Freddie's and Sandra's lives. For Sandra, it was a home she could call her own with Freddie. For Freddie, it was vindication that he could make it in his new life.

The couple made the necessary improvements to the grounds, trimmed the trees and bushes, and built a fish pond on the property. Freddie put up walls inside the outbuilding on the back. Bobbie asked him if he was fixing a place for her, but Freddie said, "No, I'm fixing me a place to stay when Sandra runs me out of the house."

It was a place they were more than happy to call home.

The year 2005, was another year with sadness. Bobbie's husband Lou, who Freddie had always called Lou Baby, passed away from

Vasculitis at the age of eighty-five. Lou Grattet and Bobbie were married forty-five years. A handsome man with salt and pepper hair, Lou was a kind-hearted, calm, considerate man who loved helping others. His work in various paper mills had taken him to different parts of the country, but he always found a way to keep in touch with family because family was so important to him. Then at the age of sixty-three, Lou retired so that he could spend more time helping family and friends. Freddie didn't talk about the loss much, but he hurt, especially for Bobbie.

As if this wasn't bad enough, Freddie suffered the loss of Pearl and Ruby not long after Lou's passing. Although Pearl and Ruby were American Tree and Feist mixed dogs, to Freddie, they were his children. They often accompanied him on visits around the community, and it was easy to see just how attached he was to them.

Sandra jokingly complained that she used to be number one before they came along. Pearl slept on the foot of the bed with Sandra and Freddie, while Ruby was content to sleep in her kennel kept inside the house.

They always turned the dogs out at night before bedtime, and this night was no different. The dogs came back in. Ruby went to her kennel, and Pearl jumped up on the bed.

Sandra noticed the foaming at Pearl's mouth. She asked Freddie what was wrong with her, and Freddie recognized it right away. Pearl had been poisoned. Sandra went to check on Ruby and noticed the same foam coming from her mouth.

Freddie took Pearl outside. With tears in his eyes, he brought her suffering to an end. He then went inside to get Ruby from her kennel, but by the time he picked her up, she was already gone.

The losses were hard for Freddie. He cried tears of sadness along with tears of anger. He saw how his beloved puppies had fallen victim to deliberately placed poison on the hunting club land directly behind his house. Whether the poison had been placed there for coyotes or stray dogs, it didn't matter to Freddie. It shouldn't have been there. He made numerous calls to the land management company complaining, but all that did was make it very clear that he was upset about it.

Life had to go on. He had to find a way to turn things around. Freddie wanted to become a responsible citizen, and he wanted a say in how things were done. He wanted to be able to vote. In order to do that, he had to have his rights restored, which meant petitioning the Governor's Clemency Board. Numerous people wrote letters on Freddie's behalf.

A letter from a former neighbor, Mrs. Barbara McCurdy, stated how she had known Freddie since he was a child, but it had been within the past five years that she came to look at Freddie and Sandra as family. The Freddie Crow she knew talked openly and honestly about the mistakes he had made, not blaming anyone but himself. She described how he tried to make up for the wrongs he had committed.

She went on to write how her husband had become disabled, and Freddie took the time to mow her grass, grate her road, fix things that needed repairing, and sit with Mr. McCurdy from time to time. In addition, Freddie prepared meals he thought Mr. McCurdy would like and shared fresh vegetables with him out of his garden. It was easy to see why Mrs. McCurdy thought of Freddie and Sandra as family.

Another letter was written by Reverend Janet Lee of the Century United Methodist Church. Reverend Lee recognized Freddie's generosity and how helpful he was to people. She pointed out that Freddie was "deliriously happy being married," and how willing he was to express his friendship with others in tangible ways. Reverend Lee wrote that it was a joy to know Freddie Crow.

Even with the glowing remarks, Freddie didn't get a good vibe when he talked about his chances of getting his rights restored with the people in the Parole Examiner's Office. Offering encouragement didn't seem to be part of their job.

Regardless, he pursued his petition. On June 15, 2006, Freddie and Sandra Crow appeared before Governor Jeb Bush and his Cabinet to request the restoration of Freddie's rights. Freddie wasn't hopeful, but he had decided that if he didn't get his rights back, it would only be because they wouldn't give them back and not because he didn't ask. To say he was nervous would be an understatement.

Freddie and Sandra watched as request after request was denied, and then it was Freddie's turn. He spoke of his mistakes, of the harm he had brought to his family, to his friends, and to himself. He talked about why he wanted his rights restored and how he wanted to be a productive member of society. He told the Cabinet about how he owned his own business and how they had recently purchased their own home. Then he talked about Sandra and just what she meant to him, how much he loved her, and how he wanted to take care of her.

Governor Bush said, "I'd like to hear from the little lady with you."

That request gave Sandra the opportunity to talk about the Freddie Crow she knew, the kind and compassionate man who was always willing to help his neighbors.

When Sandra had finished, it was time for the governor and Cabinet to vote. The governor could end it all by voting no, but if Freddie was to get his rights restored, then it would require a yes vote from the governor and at least two cabinet members.

As it turned out, Governor Bush voted yes. Attorney General Charlie Crist voted yes. Chief Financial Officer Tom Gallagher voted yes. Commissioner of Agriculture Charles Brunson voted yes. It was unanimous to restore Freddie's rights to the extent they could be restored. The right to possess a gun was not within the governor's power, though.

Freddie thanked the governor and Cabinet and then excused himself to the lobby where he grabbed Sandra and wept. Putting into words just what this meant to him was difficult. To him, it was more than having some of his rights restored; it was a vote of confidence from some of the most important people in the state. He knew God had forgiven him, but he wanted the forgiveness from the people as well, and this felt like that.

Once he was able to compose himself, Freddie's first act was to call Bobbie to let her know. During that conversation, the tears flowed again. It was a very good day.

Freddie got back to work and life. He had continued to stay in touch with Ed Hudson, and Ed with him. Although Ed truly liked Freddie as a person, their relationship was professional. Freddie told the most interesting stories, and they discovered they shared common interests in fishing and gardening.

Ed's early interviews with Freddie at the sheriff's office provided insight into what a drug dealer *really* was. He studied the way Freddie acted, talked, and thought because Freddie Crow was about as successful a drug dealer as Ed had ever known. He was also pretty sure that if an old country boy like Freddie Crow could buy and sell drugs, Ed could play the part as well. The difficult job of undercover work seemed to be much easier with this mindset.

In 2004, Ed had been promoted to Special Agent Supervisor, so the days of undercover deals were gone. However, the days of Freddie's usefulness were in full swing.

Ed waited to see if Freddie would be contacted to fly another load, giving them more information they could use for more cases. When nothing materialized, Ed notified the Office of Statewide Intelligence (OSI) at FDLE that Freddie was available if needed for a sit-down interview.

Inspector Jeff Beasley with OSI was the first to interview Freddie. It was a recap of Freddie's case with emphasis placed on his entry back into the country when flying the plane. Jeff needed to know what Freddie had to offer in the way of intelligence and investigations.

Ed called Freddie and asked him how he felt about talking with them. He explained, "They just want to pick your brain."

Freddie asked. "Are you going to be there?"

"Yes, I'll be there."

"I want to do anything that can help," Freddie stated with conviction.

Ed realized that Freddie meant it when he had said, "If there's anything you need, just let me know."

So, Ed arranged for the interview. After it was over, a decision was made to document Freddie as a confidential source (CS).

In addition to O.S.I., more law enforcement agencies requested interviews as word got out that Ed was in touch with Freddie Crow. Then a request came from the Department of Homeland Security (DHS) for an interview. Ed called Freddie to see if he would talk to them.

Freddie asked, "Reckon what they want? Are you going to be there?"

Once again, Ed assured him he would.

Freddie replied, "Then I'll do it if you're going to be there."

The meeting was set, and the interview was conducted. Freddie told his story concerning his flights, where they went, and any troubles he encountered. The DHS placed significant attention on the longitude and latitude lines used.

Freddie gave the agents an overview of the entire case that included how the organization stole airplanes. Those that sat fueled up at an unguarded airport were just waiting for someone with a manufacturer's key to come steal them and use them for any manner of criminal activity.

Then by the questions the investigators asked, Ed got the impression they were looking for a hole in the radar coverage. What they didn't seem prepared to hear was the fact that Freddie and Billy Dekle had flown so low over the water that they were able to avoid radar detection altogether.

At the end of the meeting, Ed asked if they got what they needed. The agents seemed very pleased with the results, smiling and nodding excitedly in approval.

Ed then asked the agents, "Were you more or less concerned with the flight path?"

They nodded. One of them answered, "Yes."

"Were you not concerned with how easy it was to steal an airplane?"

They didn't reply, and the interview was over. Ed was later informed that President Obama was briefed on the interview, something Ed teased Freddie the Republican about for years to come.

It was during these interviews that Ed began to pick up on a personality trait of Freddie's—he was obsessed with scheduling. When Ed called him about an interview, a date and time would be set. That was normal, but then before that confirmation call ended, Freddie repeated the day, time, and place as much as three more times. That still wasn't enough for Freddie. He was just as likely to make two more phone calls before the meeting to confirm.

Freddie continued to work and bring more good people into his life. He had a chance meeting at a Tom Thumb convenience store with Mike Merritt, an exterminator who carried a specific sprayer on the back of his pickup truck.

Freddie asked him questions about the sprayer, and a conversation started. He was looking for a sprayer to spray his house and do his own exterminating.

As usual, Freddie told Mike who he was and the bad things he had done. It was like he was apologizing for his behavior in advance.

Mike said, "I really don't care about what you've done as long as you aren't doing it now." He then pointed at his sprayer and said, "I've got a B&G sprayer like this one that I'm not using at my house if you want it. This sprayer usually sells for over two-hundred dollars, but I'll give it to you for a hundred dollars."

Freddie took him up on his offer. Not only was he able to buy the sprayer for half-price, but Mike gave him enough ingredients to spray his house three times.

That conversation began a friendship that would have Freddie and Sandra invited to events where Mike's daughters would sing. Mike was added to the long list of people Freddie would call just to check on.

During the first event where Mike's daughters were singing, Freddie asked Mike to spray his house. Mike agreed and then offered to buy back the B&G sprayer, but Freddie put on his serious face and said, "No, I might want to make me some money with it." He then gave a big smile and laughed.

Mike became a regular recipient of Freddie's vegetables as well. Freddie would sack up tomatoes, potatoes, or whatever he had at the time, and ride down to any given location in Pensacola and call Mike from his cell phone. What Mike found interesting was that Freddie would call from only two door downs from where Mike would be spraying a house, yet Freddie had no previous knowledge of where that would be at that specific moment. He did this at least ten times. Mike began to look at their relationship as one with divine intervention.

Everything was going great until October 2013. Freddie began to have pain in his right side. He told Sandra about it, and she could only tell him what it was not—his appendix or his gallbladder—and that he just needed to go to the doctor.

Freddie said, "You're my doctor."

"But I'm not a doctor, Freddie. I'm a nurse."

And because she was a nurse, she was very worried. She knew enough to know it could be serious. She was afraid for what they might find out, but at the same time, she needed to know.

Finally, an appointment was made with a gastroenterologist, and the test confirmed that Freddie had cancer on his liver. The news from the doctor was very sobering—Freddie was given six months to a year.

The news took their breath away. Then Sandra gathered up strength from deep inside her and looked the doctor straight in the eye. "It ain't over until God says it's over."

Chapter 12

The Road Home

The days following the diagnosis were filled with contradiction. Freddie had the desire to live life to the fullest, if not for himself, then for Sandra, while all the time living with the realization that he was traveling on the road that would take him to the end.

He continued to raise his garden and share his vegetables with his friends. Banana pudding was made and delivered. He planned the future for his fish pond, which required spreading dirt and restocking. He sold some of his possessions, such as his motorcycle and Volkswagen Jetta convertible, because Sandra would be able to use the money more than she would these items. Mixed in were the numerous doctor visits and decisions regarding treatment.

Freddie had so many things to do in preparation for the end, but the most pressing was to notify those he loved the most of what was to come. With each call, each visit, came the same sad story with new tears.

There is something about the impending end that can bring one to their knees. Those who would be left behind were a concern.

In Freddie's case, he spent a lot of time concerned for Sandra. Numerous hours were spent discussing these apprehensions with her and trusted friends.

One such visit came with Bobby Simpson. Freddie asked Bobby, "What would you do if you were told you had one year to live?"

Bobby thought for a minute and then replied, "I would do four things—get right with God, make apologies to those I had offended, make sure my family was taken care of, and cry."

As tears began to well up in Freddie's eyes, he said, "I've cried."

Inevitably, he thought about life after death. This was something he and Ed had often discussed at length. On one occasion, Freddie expressed concern that the life he had lived and the things he had done would prevent him from entering heaven. Although Freddie was a Christian, the devil crept in at times and left him doubting his salvation as he does with most of us from time to time.

Ed assured him, "Never listen to anyone who casts doubt about your salvation because in essence, they're saying the blood that Jesus Christ shed for us is not sufficient, and we know better than that, don't we?"

Freddie looked at Ed and said, "Yes, we do."

Ed went on to talk to Freddie about how we are all broken, and no one gets to judge our salvation but our heavenly Father. We confess our sins to Him, and His grace is all we need.

After that, Freddie never expressed any more doubt.

While there would be moments of sadness, Freddie talked about what was to come. He would begin with "I know I'm ready to go," and then end with "I just worry about Sandra." Then he'd wipe tears from his eyes.

Sandra continued to try to work as much as she could, but the time came when Freddie had so many doctor visits that she had to have help. She depended on Freddie's friend Malet Roland, his barber Paul Rudd, and Ed Hudson to take him to appointments.

Even through the pain and the doctor visits, Freddie kept his humor. Ed had taken him to one where Freddie's stomach was swollen. He was going to have a needle injected into it to draw out the fluid. Freddie tried his best not to show the apprehension he had over having a needle inserted into his stomach, but Ed could tell it was bothering him on the drive there.

Freddie was called back as Ed sat in the waiting room and prayed. Not long afterward, Freddie came back out and announced that he had good news and bad news. The good news was, they didn't have to stick him with a needle. Then in his best disgusted voice, he said, "The bad news is, I'm fat!"

Ed just laughed and said, "I guess it could be worse."

Through much of this time, Freddie maintained his network of friends either by a call or in person. He regularly visited Mike Godwin and convenience store owner Butch Watson. He enjoyed Butch's company for his ability to fix anything, but he also shared long conversations with Butch's wife Mary. She served as a spiritual inspiration to him, and Freddie was in need of that.

Mike was retired from the Florida Highway Patrol, but he and Freddie shared a common interest in airplanes. Mike was also a crop-duster and had a Cessna 206. He invited Freddie and Sandra to go flying so that he could give Freddie one last chance in the air. Mike's wife Renee stayed on the ground taking pictures as Freddie, Mike, and Sandra took off with Freddie at the wheel.

Once in the air, Mike turned around to Sandra, giving her a thumbs up. "He's still got it."

It was a wonderful memory for all, especially Freddie since he wouldn't be able to pilot any more flights. Of all the things he mostly liked about Butch and Mike was the way they were always willing to help people. He often complained to Ed that Butch could be ornery at times, and Mike could be hard-headed, but Ed could clearly to see he thought a lot of them. He talked about them often and knew if he had something that needed repaired, they would be there to help. Their only payment would be Freddie sharing his vegetables.

He also wanted to make frequent stops to see Paul Rudd at the barber shop. Freddie tried to treat everyone as good as he could, but Paul Rudd was one of the special ones who was given a nickname: "Ruddy Dudd."

Freddie also had extra special friends, long-time friends who had been with him through the years. One of them was Wayne Simpson, of course, who lived next door. Wayne was also in bad health, and Freddie often expressed concern for him. Somehow, the two ending up as neighbors and looking after one another in the end was fitting. Wayne's condition was one that was helped by the use of marijuana, so he would discreetly maintain a supply for his condition. As Freddie began to deteriorate, he made afternoon visits to see Wayne. Together, they tried to find relief for their pain.

Rocky LeBlanc was another long-time friend; however, it was often hard to tell they were friends. Rocky made frequent trips from Mobile to visit Freddie. Their conversations often consisted of long, drawn-out arguments that would be about the price of gas in Mobile, the price of rice in China, or something similarly important. Many of their conversations on the phone ended by one hanging up on the other. No concern was ever given because they both knew they would be talking again by the end of the day.

During one visit, Freddie, Rocky, Ed, and a friend of Ed's, Jay Camac, went to a local diner for lunch. They hadn't been there long when Rocky made a statement about what company supplied the food they were eating.

Freddie replied, "Oh, you think you know everything."

Rocky replied, "Well, I guess I know something about this!"

And the fight was on.

As the argument progressed, people turned their chairs to watch with amusement.

Eventually, Ed interrupted them. "Exactly how long have you two been married?"

They both sat up in their chairs, looking at one another with indignation. Then Rocky said, "A long time," for which Freddie added, "Apparently too long." Their relationship was like no other with a love seldom matched.

Freddie also had meetings between one-time adversaries. Willie Ray Thomas, a retired lieutenant with the Escambia County Sheriff's Office, was at Ed's house one day when Freddie dropped by. Willie Ray had lived in Century his whole life and spent a great deal of his career working out of the Century substation. The two knew one another, but for obvious reasons, hadn't spent much time together.

They talked for just under an hour, and in that time, the conversation turned to Freddie's diagnosis. When it was time to go, the one-time adversaries hugged.

Willie Ray said, "I love you, Freddie," and Freddie replied, "I love you, Ray."

Ed retired from the Florida Department of Law Enforcement in October 2014. As time went on, he expressed a desire to be there for Freddie, and Freddie found that he could count on Ed.

Freddie reacted very well to people who had compassion. Ed knew Freddie was dying, and he couldn't do anything to stop it, but he could walk with him through this journey. Each step of the way drew them closer and closer, so their relationship had grown to a brotherly love. They visited each other often. Freddie had always said to drop by anytime but just call first because he wanted to be sure to be there.

Everything still had to be planned out. No matter if it was a visit, a trip to the doctor, or just going out to lunch, there must first be a day, then a time, and the time needed to be pretty precise. Once these plans were set forth, Freddie always repeated them before the conversation was finished. He continued to be regimented almost to the point of being funny.

This planning sometimes came into conflict with how Sandra wanted to do things. One day when Freddie came to visit Ed, he could tell Freddie was agitated. They were walking in the back yard when Freddie said, "That Sandra!"

Ed asked, "What now?"

Freddie then went on to rant about how he and Sandra had a trip planned to Pensacola. They had specific stops they had to make while there, and then they were coming back home.

The problem came when after they arrived in Pensacola. Sandra began to think of other stops to make. Ed just listened and let Freddie talk. He continued to complain about how they had a plan, and they were supposed to stick to it.

Once everything was out of his system, Freddie paused, then turned to Ed. In the sincerest of voices, he said, "But I'm so lucky to have her. I just can't believe how lucky I am." There was no doubt that Freddie loved Sandra.

Although time for Freddie began to draw close, the time for Esta Mae was arriving much sooner. She had reached eighty-two years of age when complications from COPD caused her to check into the hospice ward at West Florida Hospital.

Freddie wasn't able to visit much, but Esta Mae informed Sandra she had something she wanted to tell him. So, he made one more trip to the hospital.

Esta Mae was lying flat on her bed watching as Freddie rubbed her feet. He said, "I heard you wanted to tell me something."

Esta Mae replied, "Yes, there is. I want you to get closer to the Lord."

Freddie took his hand and wiped his forehead. With a big grin, he said, "Whew! I thought you were going to tell me to be good to your daughter."

With that, Esta Mae rose partially from her bed, pointed her finger at Freddie, and said, "That too!"

Esta Mae Cartwright passed away on July 8, 2015. This passing represented a huge loss for Sandra, Freddie, and all of her family and friends, but Freddie knew he would see her soon.

As Freddie began to get weaker, Ed had become convinced that God had placed him there with Freddie for a reason. He was doing more than helping Freddie; he was serving his Lord. Although he couldn't take Freddie's pain away, he could be at his side and let him know he cared.

Ed would stop by and take him for a ride just to get him out of his house. Those rides turned into visits to various friends' homes just so Freddie could check on them.

The last trip Ed took him on was to a neighbor's home who had lost his son to illness. Freddie was in considerable pain, but he just wanted his neighbor to know how sorry he was.

For Freddie, friendship was about more than just good times; it was an obligation he didn't take lightly. If several days ever passed without reaching out to someone, then the call would always begin with an apology for not calling sooner.

He had a deep compassion for his friends and family, and it was his way of making sure those he cared about were okay. Even after Freddie could no longer leave home, he would think of someone who was going through a difficult time and call them up just to let them know he cared about them.

On one occasion, Freddie asked Ed to help repair a storm door at his home. By this time, Freddie had reached a point where he couldn't sit up for very long at a time. The door was repaired with a new screen.

Sandra needed a blind installed in a window, so that was taken care of along with the screen. Ed was about to leave when he noticed Sandra trimming the crepe myrtles in the yard, so he postponed his departure and finished them for her.

Freddie was able to get out of bed just as Ed was completing the work. They talked for a while next to Ed's truck. Then as Ed was about to pull away in his truck, Freddie said, "Look in your console."

Ed complied and found two twenty-dollar bills that Freddie had placed there. He wished he hadn't done that, but neither of them was in any condition to argue. Ed knew he would never be able to spend that money because those twenty-dollar bills represented payment for what Ed had done for him, but Ed didn't want money for helping. The money couldn't be used for Ed's personal gain. It was as if Freddie was giving him one last task to do—find a use for the money, and some thought would need to be given as to what that would be.

So Ed shut the lid and drove off.

Everyone's desire was to have Freddie stay at home as long as possible. So, as time grew closer to the end, Bobbie, the one person who had been with Freddie from the beginning, came to stay with him to help. Freddie declared to people that Bobbie was the sweetest woman ever. Then with a twinkle in his eye, he admonished his listener to never tell her he said that.

They had a bond held tight by love. In addition to losing her mother at such an early age, Bobbie had already seen so much death in her life—her son, her husband, her father, and countless relatives and friends. Now she had to endure losing another person who held so much of her heart. Still, she remained thankful for having them all in her life. Even with Freddie so close to death, she carried no bitterness because she knew she was a blessed woman.

Freddie had another visitor, Bobbie's daughter Darlene whom he loved dearly. Earlier, her protectiveness over her mother challenged her love for him because Bobbie and her children were Darlene's world. In the end, however, love always won out. So, Darlene came carrying a double burden of caring and concern for both Bobbie and Freddie.

So once she arrived, the deep love the two felt for the other didn't go unnoticed. It was evident in the way they treated one another.

During one of Freddie's last nights at home, he sat at the end of the kitchen bar while Darlene painted her fingernails. Once she finished, she reached over and grabbed Freddie's hand. Darlene then proceeded to paint the nail of Freddie's middle finger. Freddie got a kick out of showing everyone his painted fingernail.

The time came when all one could do was come spend a little time with Freddie to let him know he was loved, and many did that. The desire to keep him at home was beginning to become overrun with the inability to care for him. The realization came late one night when Freddie had gotten up out of bed only to sit down in a nearby chair. He wasn't able to get back up. As hard as Sandra, Bobbie, and Darlene tried, they weren't able to lift him up. Sandra called Ed, who came and managed to get him back into the bed. The next morning, the decision to call hospice was made.

That day was among the saddest. Freddie had become extremely weak. His complexion was ghostly and his cheeks sunken in. He was in pain, and no one could really do anything but wait on hospice. Sandra was on the phone trying her best to work out the details with them along with calling friends and family to let them know what was going on.

Bobbie spent a lot of time in the yard, walking out by the pond and mourning. Darlene would check on Freddie and then walk away in grief. With a heavy heart, Ed came to sit with Freddie until hospice personnel arrived, trying his best to bring some kind of comfort to him. He searched for the right words to say but found it difficult to find the right words to be supportive in such a situation.

Ed asked, "Freddie, would you like to have prayer?" The desire to pray was as much for him as it was for Freddie.

Freddie whispered, "Yes," and so for a while, they held hands and talked to God. The prayer was one of thankfulness—thanking their heavenly Father for all He had done, being thankful that we could call on Him during such difficult times, asking Him to provide comfort, first for Freddie, then to all those who loved him so much. They prayed that God would prepare each loved one for the things that were to come. Ed thanked God specifically for Freddie. He knew how rich his life had become for having Freddie in it.

When they finished praying, tears streamed down Freddie's cheeks as he took his right hand and beat his chest proclaiming, "I can feel God in me!"

Not long afterward in February 2016, as a cool wind blew, hospice arrived to take Freddie. Everyone there took their turn saying goodbye—first Bobbie, then Darlene, and then Ed—as Sandra stood to the side with tears in her eyes.

Not really knowing what to say, Ed tried to reassure Freddie that they would be able to do something for his pain.

Freddie then looked up at him and asked, "Are you coming to see me?"

Ed nodded. "I'll see you on Saturday."

Then as Freddie, the consummate planner, always did, he looked at Ed and asked, "What time?"

Wanting to laugh and cry at the same time, Ed just smiled and said, "I'll call before I come."

With that, Freddie gave him a big smile, and he was loaded into the van. Sandra got into the van with Freddie, and together they drove away, leaving behind three broken hearts.

Chapter 13

Over the Radar

The time at Joyce Goldenburg Hospice House in Pensacola was all that anyone could ask for, considering the situation. The staff was very accommodating; the room was large enough to be comfortable, and they did their best to control Freddie's pain. Even so, the days turned into nights, and the nights to days with very little differentiation, except Freddie was steadily and surely losing his life.

Each day brought new visitors. Word spreads quickly in small communities, and when the news is sad, people rise to the occasion to offer support.

Friends from childhood as well as those from later in life came to see Freddie. There just seemed to be a need to say goodbye. People like Coy and Diane Campbell, both of whom retired from the Escambia County Sheriff's Office, visited him. Coy helped tie Freddie's shoestrings together on the playground at school. He watched as Freddie's life went in a different direction than his own. Like so many others, Coy was so happy to see Freddie turn it around.

Some came to try to lift his spirits, like Wayne Simpson, Ruddy Dudd (a.ka. Paul Rudd, the barber), and Elwood Caldwell. They showed up with their middle fingernails painted red just like Freddie's and proudly displayed it for him.

Wayne returned with his brother Bobby, who shared with everyone in the room just what it was like growing up with Freddie. Others also came to share stories while others just wanted to lend support with their presence, like Butch Watson and Mike Godwin. Sandra's children—daughter Melissa with her family and son Michael—came to lend support to their mother. No one really knew what to say during this time. They just knew they cared, and they wanted to do something.

Ed Hudson kept his promise. During his first visit, Freddie was still conscious, so he spent most of the visit at Freddie's bedside. The return visits were merely to lend support to Sandra, Bobbie, and Darlene. There just wasn't anything else to do.

As the end drew near, visitation was stopped to all but family members, and Freddie was left alone with the three people who would never leave him. Freddie's nephew Bryan McElwee came one night to give aid. Concerned that Sandra had not been eating, he brought her a Mexican meal, insisting that she eat it because she knew Uncle Freddie would want her to. Bryan stayed the whole night, often finding it hard to hold back the tears.

Bobbie, Darlene, and Sandra were there until the end. When February 27, 2016, arrived, Freddie's breathing became shallower, and his heart beat slower. The hospice nurse informed the family that it wouldn't be much longer.

As the time approached, Sandra, Bobbie, and Darlene continued to stay by his side. In the afternoon hours, the breathing became so faint that the three women got on the bed with Freddie. Each proclaimed their love for him and assured him he was not alone.

Then the time came. As Freddie let go of his last breath, a tear appeared in the corner of his eye and trickled down his cheek. Freddie Crow was gone.

Ed and his wife Sharon were in Pensacola when Ed decided to call and check in. Sandra answered the phone. With a husky voice, she said, "Freddie's gone." Then he heard a soft sob.

Ed pulled over to the side of the road and cried. Once he was able to compose himself, Sharon suggested they go support his family.

They then drove immediately to the hospice house. After hugging those who were hurting so bad, Ed went into the room to say goodbye to his dear friend, who had once been so full of life. Instead, he found a lifeless body that Freddie no longer had any use for. Ed still lumbered to the bedside, his heart heavy with grief.

Although he realized the body was empty, Ed still spoke to it. "Freddie, I'm so glad you're not hurting anymore. You know I love you, and I'm going to miss you. Now, go fly over the radar all the way to heaven, and I'll see you soon."

There's sadness in any passing, but there's a comfort when you know where the person will spend eternity. Those closest to Freddie had that comfort.

Freddie's body was removed from the hospice house to be cremated. It was his wish in case Sandra never remarried. Then after she passed, he would be placed in the coffin with her. Freddie followed that wish with "If she does remarry, then just spread my ashes out in the garden."

REMEMBERING FREDDIE

Grief may be handled in different ways, but in the South, it's met with food. Tricia brought cakes. Cousin Linda brought boiled peanuts. Covered dishes came from all directions. It's just a different way to say, "I care, and I love you."

A few days went by to rest and reflect. There was no rush for the memorial service, so thought was taken in preparing it. Bobbie continued to stay with Sandra during this process.

Decisions had to be made. Chris Golden, son of the Oak Ridge Boys' William Lee Golden, and his cousin Ron Golden would provide the music and sing. Sandra asked Reverend Janet Lee and Reverend Ron Mcglothren to speak at the service.

She also asked Ed to speak. He couldn't turn her down, but he really didn't know how he could do it either. It certainly gave him something to pray about.

The memorial service was held the morning of March 9, 2016, at the Flomaton Funeral Home Chapel.

Ed spoke first. "Good morning. My name's Ed Hudson, and I'm retired after thirty-four years in law enforcement. I know many of you are wondering 'What in the world is *he* doing up there?'"

The statement was met with a good hearty chuckle from the crowded chapel. The juxtaposition of their two paths in life was not lost on those who attended. Everyone knew it was the kind of thing Freddie would've enjoyed himself.

As Ed continued to speak, there were moments of laughter and moments of tears. He spoke of Freddie's love for his dogs and his garden, about how much he loved growing vegetables and plants but equally loved sharing the bountiful harvest. Ed spoke of Freddie's love for his friends and how there were far too many to call by name, with each one having their own special Freddie Crow stories. He talked about Freddie's family, how he loved each one in his own way, and just how he cherished Sandra who was so special to him. Last but not least, Ed told those in attendance about Freddie's love for our heavenly Father.

He didn't attempt to make Freddie perfect. Freddie had made mistakes just like everyone else in the chapel because we were all broken, but he was just as well off because he was forgiven. This drew an "Amen" from Reverend Mcglothren.

Ed closed with the story of the prayer that he and Freddie shared just before he went to the hospice house and how at the end, Freddie beat his chest with tears streaming down his cheeks saying, "I can feel God in me." He told the crowded chapel that he took comfort in that, and he hoped they did as well.

The Reverends Ron Mcglothren and Janet Lee each had their own stories about Freddie to tell. Some were about Freddie in the community while others were about Freddie's interaction in church and how he loved to cook "something special" for the dinners on the grounds. Once again, tears were mixed with laughter. It was the kind of service that when people walked away from it, they thanked God for having Freddie Crow in their life.

After the service was over, many comments were made about the need for a book to be written. Chris Golden mentioned that it would be a wonderful story, sharing how two people of opposing sides had come together under the cross of Jesus.

Sandra's home was opened to friends and family afterward where many more anecdotes about Freddie were told. Ed and Sharon were among those who visited.

That afternoon, Bobbie and Sandra came to Ed with one more request. They both talked about how much they wanted a book about Freddie written. Sandra said, "Freddie had talked about writing the book, but he never was able to accomplish it." Then Bobbie added, "We think you should be the one to write it."

The first thing that entered his mind was *I know nothing about writing a book.* "I'll have to give it some thought," he told them.

Life after Freddie— Where Are They Now?

In the months and years that followed, some things had changed, and some stayed the same. Billy Dekle, who was told that the only way he would ever leave the federal prison system would be when his family came to claim his remains, benefited from a mass release of nonviolent federal prisoners. He was released on April 15, 2016.

Billy gives credit to his wife who stayed with him through it all. She told Billy of her prayers asking for his release and how she had complete faith that it would happen.

He found it hard to have that faith, though. Now he sees his release as one of divine intervention. Billy found God through his wife's faith.

Today, he spends his days at their North Florida home occupied by spending time with his grandchildren, working in his yard, grocery shopping, attending the local Baptist church, and being thankful for every minute of freedom.

Prior to Dekle's release, the prison system notified DEA Special Agent Charlie Gravat in case he had an objection. While an argument could have been made regarding the death that occurred in one of the loads and the guns in the vehicle at the time of arrest, Gravat remained silent, thinking Dekle's lesson may have been learned.

Charlie Gravat rose to the rank of Resident Agent in Charge. Then he eventually retired from the DEA in 2012, only to start working again as the head of security for a bank.

Special Agent Ron Chambers retired from the U.S. Customs Service. Sadly, he subsequently fell victim to cancer on October 23, 2017.

Randy Cannon was found dead on a dirt road not far from his home on December 30, 2019. The cause of death was multiple gunshot wounds. The investigation revealed that he had made contact with a trespasser on his property who reportedly shot Randy after being confronted.

Timothy (Timbo) Campbell still tried to learn the lesson that keeps one out of trouble. He continued to make the same mistakes and ended up back in federal prison on drug charges. July 2024 has been set as his presumptive date of release.

Bo-Bo Bell completed his sentence and entered rehab. As hard as he tried, sobriety did not come easy. He relapsed and became homeless before being rescued by his father. Bell later turned his life over to Jesus Christ and entered the ministry, which involved the Mission of Hope for the homeless along with pastoring the Church of New Beginnings Worship Center in Brewton, Alabama. In addition to all of this, Bell also owns and operates a construction company that seeks out convicted felons to hire.

Randy Hensel retired from the U.S. Attorney's Office, spending his time with family, traveling, lobstering, and ever in search of a new joke to tell.

Wayne Simpson would tell stories about Freddie until he succumbed to his illness on November 28, 2017, joining Freddie in eternity.

Bobby Simpson retired after thirty-six years of teaching high school students. His memories of Freddie remain vivid and ready to share.

Freddie's brother Hurston fought his own battle with cancer, succumbing to the damage it would do during the morning hours of March 28, 2020. Hurston was a kind man who left his mark serving the public in the U.S. Forest Service, but even more so, in being a loved man by family and friends. The times he and Freddie spent together were very cherished times.

Freddie often bragged on Tricia for her ability to make irresistible cakes, which she made for him often. She now spends her time baking cakes for various restaurants close to where she lives, but her favorite pastime is outings with her children and grandchildren.

Darlene went on to become a sales representative for Grainger Industrial Supplies while maintaining an interest in body building. She remains a guardian angel for Bobbie.

Bobbie remains thankful for all of the blessings in her life. Some days are more difficult than others when the tears keep coming, but she's still grateful for having Freddie to remember. She now lives with Darlene, and having her daughter with her helps to ease her pain.

Sandra, like Bobbie, struggles some days more than others. Anniversaries and holidays are always difficult. Some days, without explanation, the longing to see Freddie, talk to him, and touch him becomes overwhelming. She buries herself in her work and family, spending time with her daughter Melissa and her family and with her son Michael. Michael gave Sandra one of her most cherished possessions, a pencil sketch drawing of Freddie with a bi-wing plane in the background. It was such a great depiction that Sandra wanted to use it for the cover of this book about Freddie.

Family can help make the difference.

To this day, all of Freddie's friends and family members always find the time to stop what they're doing to either listen to or share a story about Freddie.

Ed learned that Freddie had studied how to write a book by reading other books about it. Sandra gave him all of Freddie's writing books along with the little bit he had written in a notebook and the documents he had submitted for public records request for transcripts. Ed was surprised at the similarity of their writing styles and voice. It was like Freddie was waiting on someone to do it.

A Note from
the Author

I think of Freddie often. Wonderful cherished memories come to mind as I continue to come across those things that Freddie enjoyed so much.

I grew scuppernongs, a type of Southern grape, in my yard, and Freddie had loved scuppernongs. But when he was still alive, they had been disappearing. Possums and coons love them too, so I put a game camera on the vines to see what had been eating them. After a few days, I saw a picture on the camera, so I checked it. I called Freddie to tell him something had showed up on the camera.

Freddie replied, "It did? What was it?"

I replied, "A Crow."

Silence.

Then I said, "I got you on the camera."

Freddie had been captured helping himself to some scuppernongs, which left both of us with a big laugh.

In August, 2016, after Freddie's death, I looked out my front window to see one lone crow jump from the ground to the vine, eating one scuppernong after another. My eyes began to water as I reminisced of those wonderful times with him. It was a happy recollection wrapped in a sad moment.

As I stand in my kitchen today, I can see Freddie sitting at the kitchen counter. One time, I had given him a pint of homemade salsa to share with Sandra. I asked, "Freddie, did you try my salsa?"

"That's been gone awhile," he answered. "It sure was good."

"Did you share it with Sandra?"

Freddie sat straight up on the bar stool, looked down at the counter, raised his eyebrows, and began rubbing the countertop with the palm of his hand in a counterclockwise motion.

I thought, *Okay, I've seen this before. He's about to confess.*

"Well," he said, still not looking at me, "I was working in the yard, and I hadn't had anything to eat all day. I decided to come in and take a break. I started eating the salsa with some chips, and before I knew it, there wasn't but just a little bit left, so I decided to just finish it off. But it sure was good."

Then just like that, Freddie stopped rubbing the countertop and looked up at me as if he was expecting punishment.

I walked to the pantry and picked up another pint of salsa. This time, I wrote "SANDRA" across the top and gave it to him.

He smiled and said, "I'll see that she gets it."

Many things remind me of Freddie, but probably nothing as much as the two twenty-dollar bills Freddie had put into my console. I was determined to find the right person or place to which I could give that money.

Then on October 7, 2018, Hurricane Michael destroyed the eastern part of the Florida Panhandle as a Category 5 hurricane. I was privileged to make several trips to the area in an effort to assist in helping people clean up their property.

In March 2019, I met Reverend Eddie Lafountain, pastor of the First Baptist Church of Mexico Beach. He had opened up his church's facilities to act as a supply distribution center to the area residents who were still badly in need of help. It was a shoestring operation that filled a very large need, and it was easy to see how overwhelming the task was.

I went back to my truck and picked up the two twenty-dollar bills. I brought them to the pastor and asked if he would accept a cash donation. I told him the story of my friend as tears came to my eyes.

After praying that the use of the money would be blessed, I left with a conviction that Freddie's story should be told. In the end, I realized it wasn't about the pilot who dared to do anything in an airplane, but it was about a man who had a mission to let people know they mattered. It was about a man who went out of his way to let people know they were loved.

So many memories of Freddie frequently crop up. Acquaintances and friends of Freddie, as well as family members, continue to tell their stories.

I have learned to call on one memory in particular when sadness comes—the prayer of thankfulness that Freddie and I prayed at his bedside just before the hospice personnel came to take him from his home. I'll never forget how when it was over, Freddie pounded his chest and said, "I can feel God in me!" It is in these words that I take comfort and hope others do as well.

About the Author

Ed Hudson grew up in the rural area of northwest Florida around the community of Walnut Hill. His youth was spent working on farms, toting bricks and blocks, making mortar for his father's masonry business, and attending Ernest Ward School. After graduating high school in 1976, with a class of forty-one students, Ed attended Pensacola Junior College where he received an associate of science in law enforcement.

In 1980, Ed graduated with a bachelor of arts in criminal justice administration from the University of West Florida and went to work with the Century Police Department. Although small with only five police officers, he gained a lot of experience at the CPD.

The year 1981 brought employment as a deputy at the Escambia County Sheriff's Department where Ed worked patrolling the highways of northern Escambia County for the next nine years. Then in 1990, he transferred to the narcotics unit. The experience he obtained from working high-level narcotics cases prepared him for a job as a special agent with the Florida Department of Law Enforcement (FDLE) starting in 1993.

Working in the Pensacola region, Ed worked a variety of cases with his fellow FDLE agents along with agents from the DEA, ATF, U.S. Customs, and Secret Service. These agents were among the finest men and women he has ever known.

Ed was promoted to Special Agent Supervisor in 2004, and remained in this position until retirement on October 1, 2014. During his time in law enforcement, Ed received numerous awards and recognition from the Escambia County Sheriff's Office, DEA, U.S. Secret Service, and the U. S. Attorney's Office for the Northern District of Florida. In 2010, Ed also received the FDLE Contribution to Criminal Justice Award for his part with the Methamphetamine Law Implementation Team.

Today, Ed spends his retirement gardening and fishing whenever possible. He enjoys time with his granddaughters, especially when fishing, and with friends if they're going fishing. He serves his community through his church, the Walnut Hill Baptist Church, and as a member of the Walnut Hill Ruritan Club, an organization that lends a hand to those in need in the community.

Then he goes fishing.

Made in the USA
Coppell, TX
06 September 2020